An 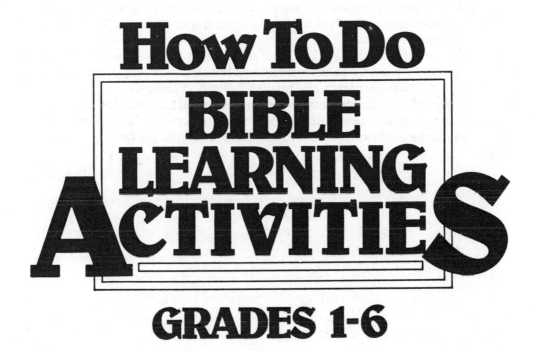 Christian Education/Christian School Resource

How To Do
BIBLE
LEARNING
ACTIVITIES

GRADES 1-6

by Barbara J. Bolton · illustrated by Catherine Leary

International Center for Learning

INTERNATIONAL CENTER FOR LEARNING
A Subsidiary of GL Publications, Ventura, California, U.S.A.

About the Author

Barbara Bolton earned a B.A. degree at Whittier College and an M.A. degree in elementary education at California State College, Los Angeles.

Her teaching career spans kindergarten through sixth grade over the past 30 years. She is a specialist in the field of remedial reading and has taught in both public and Christian schools.

Barbara is currently directing ICL's Christian school ministry. She has also served as ICL's Children's Division Coordinator. She has held nearly every office in Sunday School, including a two-year term as Christian Education Director.

As a member of the ICL seminar teams for Sunday School and for Christian schools, Barbara conducts seminars for children's teachers and leaders across the continent. She is the author of several ICL training resources for teachers and leaders.

Unless otherwise noted, Scripture quotations are from *The New American Standard Bible.* © The Lockman Foundation 1960, 1962, 1963, 1968, 1971, 1972, 1973, 1975. Used by permission.
Another version quoted is:
The New International Version, Holy Bible. Copyright © 1978 by New York International Bible Society. Used by permission.

Published by International Center for Learning
GL Publications, Ventura, California 93003.
Printed in U.S.A.

ISBN 0-8307-0850-2

WHERE TO FIND. . .

BIBLE LEARNING THAT CHANGES LIVES

The basic goal of sharing God's Word with children is that their lives will be changed as they receive Christ as Saviour and grow in Him. However, children can repeat facts without showing any evidence of changed lives.

Changed lives occur as a work of the Holy Spirit when the learner is actively involved in the process of applying Scripture to life experiences. James 1:22 tells us, "Do not merely listen to the word, and so deceive yourselves. Do what it says" (*NIV*).

This book explores ways of involving children in the learning experiences so that they will not only hear the Word, they will be drawn to God in a life-changing relationship.

In planning Bible learning activities which involve the learner, you need to consider your students' general age characteristics as well as their individual differences. If you provide a variety of learning experiences that take into account your students' various interests and abilities, both you and your students will enjoy exploring God's Word together.

To help you do this, we have grouped the activities in this book in seven categories:

1. art activities
2. drama activities
3. oral communication
4. creative writing
5. music activities
6. research activities
7. Bible games.

Meaningful Choices

Children enjoy learning more when they can make choices and feel successful in what they are doing. Children tend to select activities that utilize their strengths. However, over a period of time, they will usually select a good balance of activities. They enjoy trying new things. Their thinking will thus be stretched.

The key to providing choices is the word MEANINGFUL! All choices must be related to the Bible truth being studied. In 2 Timothy 2:15 we read, "Be diligent to present yourself approved to God as a workman who does not need to be ashamed, handling accurately the word of truth." This is our charge. The choices we provide for children MUST be related to Bible truth.

Life Application

Life application is another MUST! Changed lives happen when the learner applies the Bible truth to his daily life—when he makes decisions based on what God's Word says.

God tells us His Word will thoroughly equip us for living. "You, however, continue in the things you have learned and become convinced of, knowing from whom you have learned them; and that from childhood you have known the sacred writings which are able to give you the wisdom that leads to salvation through faith which is in Christ Jesus. All Scripture is inspired by God and profitable for teaching, for reproof, for correction, for training in righteousness; that the man of God may be adequate, equipped for every good work" (2 Tim. 3:14-17).

Research Skills

Research is an essential part of Bible learning activities. You can help children develop good research skills as they look for information. They can do some research independently. At other times, they will need to interact with teachers and other children.

The Bible should be the child's prime source of information. Encourage your students to read and talk about Bible verses related to the unit of study. Provide Bible verses on tape for those who have difficulty reading.

Other resources you can provide are books, pictures, slides, films, filmstrips, models, Bible maps and atlases, Bible dictionaries and concordances. Children enjoy viewing filmstrips/slides and listening to tapes at viewing/listening centers. The use of headsets allows children to listen to a tape without disturbing others.

Learning Environment

In order to provide work space for a variety of Bible learning activities, you need a room arrangement that is FLEXIBLE! Tables and chairs do move! Use the floor area. Children can accomplish most activities on the floor as easily as they can sitting in chairs at tables. If space is a problem, more may be created by removing unnecessary furniture.

The general appearance of the room needs to be neat and orderly. Maximum learning does not occur in a clutter. Children can accept the responsibility for putting things away and caring for their room.

From time to time you may want to change your room arrangement.

Supplies

Sometimes teachers do not involve children in Bible learning activities because the materials they need to use are not readily available. Here are some basic supplies you'll want to have on hand:

poster board	stapler and staples
assorted construction paper	scissors
newsprint or chart paper	glue and paste
drawing paper	tape—transparent and masking
pencils	paper clips
water colors	paper fasteners
tempera paint	boxes
paint brushes	fabric and scraps for costumes
felt pens	shelf or butcher paper
crayons	clay and/or dough
chalk	magazine pictures
sponges	

A secondary supply list might include such items as:

wire hangers	meat trays
string	clothespins
wax paper	paper plates

sandpaper	paper bags
chalk	egg cartons
tissue paper	liquid starch
cellophane	cleanup supplies
chenille wire	plastic containers
yarn	starch

Check your curriculum materials for any additional supplies you may need.

There is no one best way to organize supplies. The important thing is to develop a plan that will:
- work in the available space;
- involve learners in its maintenance;
- not require hours and hours of work.

You may wish to establish a central supply area to be used by all the classes in the building. If you do, someone will need to accept the responsibility for organizing and maintaining the area. No one's responsibility is somehow never accomplished!

The supply person should be responsible for the inventory and purchase of needed supplies. He/she should prepare a list of basic supplies, using an order form format. Provide space for listing special supplies and the dates they are needed. Pad copies of the order form and distribute them to teachers and other workers. Those who need to have supplies purchased can complete this order form and give it to the supply person.

When one person buys all the supplies, you can take advantage of bulk-purchase discounts and avoid wasteful duplications.

Some of the supplies you need are in the drawers and on the shelves of every household. Print in your church or school newsletter or bulletin a list of items you need. Parents and other interested people will be glad to supply greeting cards, bits of fabric and yarn, egg cartons, etc., etc., etc.

Selecting and Planning Activities to Provide

Based upon your knowledge of your learners' needs and the Bible truths they will be studying, select the *activities you will make available*.

Learners should be given choices *of* activities and also choices of *how to complete* activities. For example, they may:
- choose from several kinds of materials;
- decide upon the content of the activity;
- determine the best way to share their research.

Be sure to plan for a variety of activities. A very effective learning activity that is used too frequently becomes less and less effective. From time to time check to see that you are providing activities from all of the seven categories in this book.

Guiding Learners in Choosing Activities

A simple, effective way to guide learners in their choice of activities is to prepare a chart listing all of the activities available. Cut strips of construction paper—a different color for each activity. Provide as many strips of each color as there can be children involved in the activity—no more than eight children per activity.

Briefly explain each activity. Tell children to think about two activities they would like to work on in case they don't get their first choice. Ask who wants to choose each activity. Give appropriate colored strips to those who volunteer for each activity. Ask learners to write their names on their slip of paper and paste it by the title of the activity they chose.

Here's another way to make a choice chart: Attach library pockets to a piece of poster board—one pocket for each activity. Put strips of colored paper in each pocket—a different color in each pocket. Limit the number of strips to the number of children who can work on that activity. Children indicate their choice of activity by removing a colored strip from the appropriate pocket, writing their name on it and putting it back in the pocket.

Make it clear that choosing to not participate is *not* an option! Children need to choose one activity. They will usually be eager to select an activity if there are some choices in ways of completing it. However, occasionally a learner may have some difficulty making a choice.

If this happens, be sure to explain the procedure again. Walk from activity to activity and observe for a few minutes. Answer questions the learner might ask. If the child still has difficulty making a decision, say something like, "We really need another person to help with the mural." Or, "You need to make a choice within the next three minutes. If you would like, I will help you with the choice."

Children need to be encouraged to "stick with" an activity until they have completed it. There may be some exception to this if they have a special need or if they make a poor choice and learning is not happening.

Directions Are the Key!

Directions must be clear and concise. Tell only as much as the learner needs to know in order to do the next step. Most first, second and third graders need to hear *one* direction at a time. Usually, fourth, fifth and sixth graders can hear, remember and follow two or three directions.

It is helpful to ask a learner to repeat the directions. This enables you to make sure the learners heard what you think you said. Also, learners will benefit from hearing another child state the directions.

Adults need to be consistent with expectations and follow-up of directions. Wait until one set of directions has been followed before giving additional directions.

Teachers using a learning center approach may need to prepare some directions that can be followed independently. Younger children often need help with an activity. Let's look at several ways to prepare directions so that children can use them without the help of an adult.

When did it happen?
1. Look at the pictures
2. Hang them on the clothesline to show what happened first and next and next.

3. Read about one picture in your Bible.
4. Tell a friend about it.

Task cards can be prepared very quickly and easily, either by the teacher or an older student. Some words can be sketched to aid children with limited reading ability.

Letter directions on large index cards or construction paper folded into a tent shape. Place directions on the table, floor or bulletin board.

Note the simplicity of the card.

Children will enjoy following directions on a "rebus direction chart." List the steps to be followed and illustrate the words that can be pictured with a simple drawing or magazine picture.

The tape recorder is an invaluable aid to the teacher who is the only adult in the room but who would like to guide children to work independently for a portion of time. Reading or talking ideas and directions into a tape recorder is a simple task that will not require too much teacher preparation time. Read through the following script. Adapt it to give directions to some of your learners.

Obey Your Parents—a sample Bible learning activity script

How to use the cassette tape
1. Use the tape with headsets or play it softly without headsets.
2. To avoid discussion about which child will operate the tape player, put a piece of masking tape on one of the chairs. The child sitting on that chair may operate the tape player.

Preparation for younger children
1. Letter "Ephesians 6:1" on a card or nearby chalkboard so children can look at this reference while locating the verse in their Bibles.
2. Put a drop of green paint on the play button of the tape player and a drop of red paint on the stop button.

Sample script
God loves us so much that He has planned for us to live in families. People in a family work and play together. Let's read a Bible verse that will tell us how God wants us to get along with our parents. Open your Bibles to just a little space before the end. Find Ephesians 6:1. The name of the book is Ephesians. The number of the chapter is 6 and the number of the verse is 1. When you are ready to look for Ephesians 6:1, turn off the tape recorder. When you have found this verse, turn the tape recorder on again. (Pause 10 seconds.)

Now that you have found Ephesians 6:1, let's read it together, "Children, obey your parents in the Lord, for this is right." Think about what this verse is saying. To obey our parents in the Lord means that it is God's plan for us to do what our parents tell us as they are directed by God.

Sometimes our parents ask us to do things that we don't want to do right away. For example, when it's bedtime and we're busy doing an interesting project, we don't want to stop right away and go to bed. Or, if our parents say it's time to turn off the TV and practice a piano lesson, we might not really want to do it. God knows that we need to have guidance and direction from our parents. Sometimes it's easy to follow this direction and other times it's not.

In just a minute, turn off the tape recorder and share with each other about a time when it's *easy* for you to obey your parents. Remember that each person in the group needs to have a turn to tell about just *one* time when it's *easy* for you to obey your parents. When you have all had a turn, turn on the tape recorder. (Pause 10 seconds.)

Now let's think about a time when it's more difficult to obey. Turn off the tape recorder and each person tell about one time it's *difficult* for you to obey your parents. When each person has had a turn, turn on the tape recorder. (Pause 10 seconds.)

Now we're going to work together to make a parallel frieze. A parallel frieze is a long strip of shelf paper that has two rows of pictures. One row shows one idea and the other row shows another idea. When we look at the pictures, we can compare the two ideas.

Our frieze needs to have some pictures that show times when it's *easy* to obey and pictures that show times when it's *hard* to obey. You may draw several pictures. Someone in the group can letter Ephesians 6:1 on the shelf paper. You may use drawing paper and felt pens to make your drawings.

If you have questions about what you are going to do, you may ask your teacher. Turn off the tape recorder while you are working. This is the end of the tape."

Continued guidance

Post a chart listing the steps to follow so that children can continue to be relatively independent as they draw. Observe the children's work and guide their conversation about obedience as they make their pictures and attach them to the strip of paper.

Preparing a tape

Tape recordings may also be used to give information rather than directions.

When making tapes, it is helpful to write out the script. Read it slowly. Pause for about 10 seconds at the places where the tape recorder is being turned off and then on again. This will prevent losing a portion of the words.

You will enjoy using the tape recorder to help children gain independence as they work and to increase the variety of resource materials. However, it cannot replace the warm, loving interaction that learners need with their teachers.

Working Together

Following are five simple steps that need to be taken for the completion of a meaningful Bible learning activity. Your lesson plan can be developed around these five steps. Evaluate each one as you move through the process.

1. Learner-teacher planning

It's important for learners and teachers to plan together at the beginning of the activity. Answer these three questions.
● What are we going to do?
● What do we need to know in order to do it?
● How will we do it? (Include who will do each part)

Record answers on chalkboard or chart paper so children can refer to their plan while they are working.

2. Research

This step will answer the question "What do we need to know in order to do it?" The Bible should be a prime resource for every activity. Also use other books,

10

pictures, slides, filmstrips, records, tapes, field trips, resource people, etc. Be creative. Use a wide variety of resources.

3. Do it!
Make a specific plan that will answer these two questions: Who will do what? How will we do it?

Execute the plan. Assist the children in gathering the supplies. Follow the group plan for doing the activity. Talk about the Bible truths and information as children work. Allow children to accept as much responsibility for work as possible. They are not onlookers while the teacher does the activity. The teacher is the facilitator.

Continue the research process throughout the activity. Ideas, attitudes and feelings are stretched as children gain new information and incorporate it into their thinking and actions.

4. When appropriate, plan a way to share the activity with others
The activity can be shared with the rest of the class or with another class or with parents and friends. The best way to share an activity depends on what the activity is. You might plan a special time for showing the results of the activity. Or, the project may lend itself to being displayed on a bulletin board or wall.

Remember that the finished product is not as important as the process that brought it about. The purpose of Bible learning activities is to cause learning to happen as children study God's Word, interact with each other, with their teacher and with other resources.

5. Follow-up
To insure the application of Bible truths in daily life situations, you and your learners need to continue to interact about the information, understandings and feelings that result from the process of the activity.

You may wish to telephone a child to ask how he/she is doing with the idea of obeying parents or showing love to people he/she is just becoming acquainted with—or whatever the Bible truth is that the children are studying. A note mailed to the child can be a great encouragement. Conversation and other communication with parents will make it possible for parents to reinforce the learning.

Building positive, caring relationships with your learners and their families as you help them apply Bible truths in daily life will create an environment that God can use to change the lives of your students.

Working with a Slower/Disabled Learner

Some characteristics a slower/disabled learner may demonstrate:
1. Very short attention span—does not complete task; easily distracted.
2. Limited comprehension—can't recall basic facts, draw conclusions, answer questions; constantly makes inappropriate guesses.
3. Poor verbal communication skills.
4. Very easily frustrated—gives up easily.
5. Works carelessly and too fast.
6. Appears tense and uses finger to point to words while reading.
7. Holds book too close or too far away.
8. Reads word by word (short, choppy); adds/omits words.

Some tips for working with slower/disabled learners:
1. Provide smaller teacher/learner ratio. Or, have someone available to work with child individually as needed (department leader, aide, caring person who volunteers).
2. Provide structured environment (clearly-defined schedule, rules, procedures).
3. Use multi-sensory aids that make use of seeing, hearing, tasting, smelling, touching.
4. Be sensitive to child's special needs and limitations.
   - Don't call on slow reader to read out loud.
   - Give slower learner shorter, easier assignments that he/she can complete successfully. Give sincere, warm praise for these efforts.
   - Let non-readers assist in some way such as holding a picture.
5. Use direct eye contact and appropriate facial expressions.
6. Speak clearly, distinctly, not too fast. Give one direction at a time.
7. Be close enough to touch child when attention wanders.
8. Recapture attention by saying child's name or asking child's opinion.
9. Use literal, not abstract, terms.
10. Express the same idea in different words, from simple to more complex.
11. Give individualized assignments if child is extra slow.
12. Don't present too much at one time on a written page.

Working with an Advanced/Gifted Child

Some characteristics an advanced/gifted child may demonstrate:
1. Good verbal communication skills.
2. Highly motivated; completes tasks.
3. Needs a variety of experiences (intellectual—reading; creative—art, music)

Some tips for working with an advanced/gifted child:
1. Give extra assignments that make use of child's special gifts/abilities (research project; planning some part of the lessons; helping a slower learner; teaching a new song; playing an instrument; making patterns to trace; writing a play to present to another group; organizing a service project for senior citizens, the homebound, an orphanage; being chairman or recorder for a committee). Ask all of your class for *their* suggestions as to ways they can use the special abilities God has given each of them.
2. Always have extra Bible learning activities/games ready. Advanced/gifted child will complete more, faster than other children do.

Grade-Level Symbol Used in This Book
Each Bible learning activity has a symbol that indicates the approximate grade level(s) for which that activity is most appropriate (adapt according to the needs/abilities of *your* learners). The darkest area indicates the most appropriate grade(s); the lighter shading indicates an additional range of appropriateness.

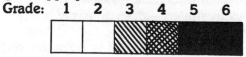

Grade: 1 2 3 4 5 6

ART ACTIVITIES

Bible learning activities involving creative art experiences provide an enjoyable and effective way for children to learn. As you use these activities, remember that the learning *process* is more important than the end *product*. As you select and use art activities, note the purpose and guided conversation ideas for each activity. These activities are not designed as craft projects, but as creative experiences that reinforce and enrich Bible learning.

Benefits

Lesson-related art activities can help a child:

- show in a concrete way an abstract concept such as loving, forgiving, worshiping, serving;
- think in terms of specifics (clean my room, take out the trash) as he/she applies a Bible verse ("Children, obey your parents.");
- discover/show new learnings (for example, illustrating in proper sequence the events of a Bible story);
- put into practice Bible truths (for example, showing love to others by making tray favors for residents in a convalescent home;
- express thoughts that may be difficult to put into words, such as illustrating a scene from a Bible story.

Tips

1. Materials for art activities are limited only by your imagination! Much of the material may be throw-away items which have been collected, labeled and stored. See list on page 6 for ideas.
2. Enlist the help of interested parents and church members in collecting and labeling these items. (List the articles in your church newsletter or bulletin.)
3. See page 6 for a list of basic supplies/equipment for art activities.
4. Store materials/equipment in an organized way where children can see and reach them. Label containers and shelves so children can easily return items to their proper places.
5. In providing research resources for use with art activities, be sure to include a wide range that will challenge children with varying abilities. See suggestions in "Research Activities" section, page 92.

ART ACTIVITIES

COLLAGE

See explanation on page 12.

Purpose: That the child express attitudes and understandings about Scripture as he/she creates a collage.

Materials
- ☐ Lightweight cardboard or construction paper
- ☐ Scissors
- ☐ Glue
- ☐ Bibles
- ☐ Pictures (optional)
- ☐ Newspapers to cover work area
- ☐ Assortment of materials that the group wishes to use (A "collage box" may contain such items as beans, buttons, greeting cards, chenille wire, bits of string, thread, yarn, toothpicks, scrap paper, cork, plastic foam, Styrofoam, feathers, cotton, straws, lace, fabric scraps, sandpaper, variety of macaroni shapes, and endless other items decided upon by the group.)

Procedure
1. Talk about the ideas to be shared by way of the collage.
2. Plan for the materials to be used. If needed items are not available in the "collage box" ask teachers, learners and parents to save or collect these items.
3. Read and talk about the related Scripture.
4. Plan (you may wish to sketch on the background) the design of the collage.
5. Use strong glue to attach the materials to the background.

Variations
1. Use burlap, muslin or other coarse fabric for the background. Sturdy paper plates and empty meat trays make satisfactory backgrounds.
2. The completed collage may be sprayed with shellac or other plastic sealer.

Guided Conversation Ideas
Ask younger children to describe the "feel" and "smell" of nature items as they make collages showing God's creation. Such collages provide pleasing dimensions for the children. Ask, "How did God plan for pine cones, seeds and nuts to continue growing many kinds of plants?" "How can we live and work in God's creation in a way that pleases Him?" "Find the verse in Genesis 1 that describes _____ ."

ART ACTIVITIES

MONTAGE

Purpose: That the child share an idea or feeling as he/she arranges pictures next to and overlapping each other on a background.

Materials
☐ Magazines
☐ Scissors
☐ Glue or paste
☐ Construction paper or lightweight poster board for background
☐ Bibles

Procedure
1. Select the idea or feeling that is to be illustrated by the montage.
2. Read and talk about related Scripture verses.
3. Cut from magazines, pictures that will help to share the idea or feeling.
4. Arrange them on the background paper, overlapping the edges.
5. When the arrangement is satisfactory, glue the pictures in place.

Variations
1. Greeting cards, original drawings and newspapers may be a source of pictures and/or letters.
2. Felt pens may be used to add lettering.
3. Younger children may make montages when the pictures are cut out of the magazines and children select those they wish to use.
4. Cut the background paper into a shape that will help to share the idea or feeling.

Guided Conversation Ideas
To teach the Bible verse "This is my command: Love each other" (John 15:17, NIV), select pictures that show ways to demonstrate love and caring. Arrange them on a heart shape. Ask, "How will you show love to someone in your family this week?" "How do you feel when the actions of a friend show love?"

MOSAIC

Purpose: That the child use small pieces of selected material to make a picture or design that will share an idea or that can be used for a gift.

Materials
- ☐ Bibles
- ☐ Cardboard for background (if materials used are heavy)
- ☐ Poster board for background
- ☐ Assorted construction paper to tear or cut into small pieces
- ☐ Assorted seeds
- ☐ Bits of fabric
- ☐ Glue
- ☐ Shellac (optional—effective if used with seeds)

Procedure
1. Read Bible verses related to the ideas shared in the picture.
2. Plan the picture or design. The child may wish to sketch it on the background.
3. Tear construction paper into small pieces. Store the pieces, sorted by color, in small plastic bags.
4. Glue the pieces in place on the background. Pieces will need to overlap in order to fill in the spaces.

Variations
1. Use paper plates or meat trays for background.
2. Attach bent paper clips for hangers and use for gifts.
3. Attach black cord to outline portions of the picture. This is effective if the areas are large, such as a group picture.

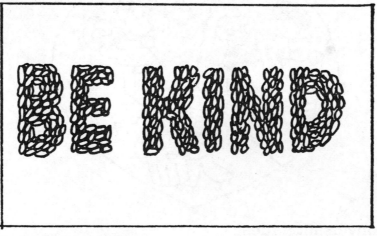

Guided Conversation Ideas
Talk about the Bible verse/story. "What part of the story can you see in the picture?" "What did _____ say about _____ ?" "What will you do this week to obey that verse?" "What did Jesus mean when He said _____ ?"

BULLETIN BOARDS

Purpose: That the child plan a way to effectively display on a bulletin board a Bible truth he has learned.

Materials
- ☐ Bibles
- ☐ Bulletin board (large butcher paper if bulletin boards are not available)
- ☐ Felt pens
- ☐ Pins or stapler and staples
- ☐ Assorted construction paper to use for backing, borders or cutout letters
- ☐ Scissors
- ☐ Pencils and paper (optional)

Procedure
1. Most often a bulletin board display will grow out of a completed project that needs to be mounted and made available for others to see.
2. Simply plan the placement of the items on the bulletin board. (Bulletin boards may be very simple—merely mount the items to display—or they may be more involved projects needing a background, title, Bible verse and/or explanatory copy.)
3. Mount items if desired.
4. Use felt pens to letter title. Or, cut letters from construction paper.

Variations
1. Plan and prepare a bulletin board that will share new ideas or reinforce or review information.
2. Bulletin boards may be used for announcements.
3. Add interest to the bulletin board with dimensional items when it is possible.

Guided Conversation Ideas
"What is the main idea that we want our bulletin board to share?" "How can we arrange things on it so that our idea is communicated?" "What Bible verse would help to share our idea?" Letter it and add to the bulletin board.

ART ACTIVITIES

REBUS

Purpose: That the child use pictures to express ideas that are part of a song or Bible verse.

Materials
- ☐ Bibles
- ☐ Chart paper, newsprint, butcher or shelf paper
- ☐ Drawing paper
- ☐ Felt pens or crayons
- ☐ Magazine pictures (optional)
- ☐ Glue
- ☐ Scissors

Procedure
1. Letter song or Bible verse on paper. Older children may do their own lettering. The teacher needs to complete the lettering prior to class time for younger children.
2. Leave blank spaces for the words that can be illustrated.
3. Each child needs to select the word(s) that he/she will illustrate.
4. Draw the pictures. (Children may work on separate sheets of paper which are then glued onto word chart.)
5. Sing the song or say the Bible verse.
6. Use the rebus during worship or sharing time.

Variations
1. Select magazine pictures instead of drawing pictures.
2. Use water color paints. The brushes are small and can be used in a small area.
3. Write a new verse for the song.

The Lord is my 🧑‍🦱.
I shall not want.
He makes me lie
down in 🌳.

He leads me beside 〰️.

Guided Conversation Ideas
"What kind of drawing can you use to show what the word _____ means?" "What are some of the other verses in the Bible that tell us the same thing?"

ART ACTIVITIES

SLIDES

Purpose: That the children prepare a slide presentation to **express their** understandings and feelings about a Bible story or a modern-day situation.

Materials
☐ Bibles
☐ Camera
☐ Slide film
☐ Slide projector
☐ Tape recorder and blank cassette (optional)

Procedure
1. Read and talk about the Bible story or the situation that the children plan to use in their presentation.
2. Make a list of the scenes needed.
3. Decide who will be in each scene.
4. Pose the scenes and take pictures (shoot several variations in each scene to allow some choice in final selection of slides).
5. Have slides developed.
6. Assemble the slides and view them.
7. Children may wish to prepare a taped narration. Or they may choose to tell about each slide as it is projected.

Variations
1. Draw pictures and then use the camera and film to take slide pictures of the drawings. This is an effective way to prepare a program that doesn't require a lot of effort on the day of the event; for example, a Christmas program in which children can sit with their parents and enjoy the presentation.
2. If slides are taken while holding the camera on its side and developers are given the instructions to *just develop* the film and *not cut* it apart and mount as slides, the result will be a filmstrip.

Guided Conversation Ideas
Talk about sequence, ie. "What happened next?" "What did he do then?" "How would Philippians 4:19 help you in this situation?" "What can you tell about this picture that will help everyone understand why that is a hard decision?" "What are two more ways to act when that happens to you?"

WRITE-ON SLIDES

Purpose: That the child share Bible story events or prepare a presentation of a modern day situation and explore alternative responses to the situation.

Materials
- ☐ Bibles
- ☐ Paper
- ☐ Pencils
- ☐ Write-on slides (Kodak Ectagraphic Write-On slides (available at some camera stores and at audiovisual suppliers)
- ☐ Fine-point overhead transparency pens (washable)
- ☐ Slide projector
- ☐ Chart for children to use as they work:
  a. On paper, trace around the edge of the slide to make a square.
  b. Draw your idea within the square. Use *simple* line drawings or lettering.
  c. Put the slide over your drawing. Work on the *dull* side of the slide.
  d. You can make changes by washing off the slide and drying it.
  e. If you wish to make the drawing permanent, spray it with hair spray.
  f. Load the projector and share your work with the group.

Procedure
1. Read and talk about the events in the Bible story.
2. List the events.
3. Have children work individually or in a small group to draw or write on the slides. Have them follow the procedure you listed on the chart (see "Materials" above).

Variations
1. Younger children may participate in this kind of activity by using blank transparencies, pens and an overhead projector.
2. Use slides as you work with responses to modern day situations: Ask children to make four slides to illustrate a situation they face today. Do not include the ending. Make three-four possible responses to the situation. Select a response that is comfortable for child.

Guided Conversation Ideas
When considering alternative responses, ask, "Why does that response feel comfortable to you?" "What might happen if you respond in that way?" "Is there a Bible verse that will help make the decision about what to do?" The group may wish to pray together about some decisions they are facing.

FINGER PAINTING

Purpose: That child express his/her ideas, feelings, knowledge about a specific topic.

Materials
☐ Powdered or liquid tempera paint
☐ Liquid starch
☐ Liquid detergent (optional)
☐ Paper with a glazed surface (butcher or shelf paper)
☐ Newsprint or newspapers to cover table
☐ Sponges and paper towels
☐ Source of water for cleanup (a bucket filled with water if sink is not available)

Procedure
1. Pour one or two tablespoons of liquid starch onto paper. Sprinkle powdered or undiluted tempera over it.
2. Children use hands to spread starch and paint over paper to make a pleasing design or simple picture. Encourage them to experiment with using different parts of their hands.

Note: Extra starch or paint may be added to maintain a workable consistency. A few drops of detergent may be added for easy cleanup.

Variations
1. Do finger painting on a smooth surface such as a tray or table top. Press clean paper on top of painting. Carefully pull off paper. Design will transfer to paper.
2. Place cutout pictures on wet painting, or paste them on when painting is dry. Also use this procedure for mural backgrounds.
3. Add coffee grounds, sawdust or sand to paint for interesting effects.

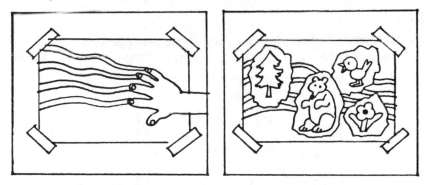

Guided Conversation Ideas
Example: To teach the Bible verse "Give thanks to the Lord, for He is good" (Psalm 106:1), use these questions/comments: "What are some different designs you can make with different parts of your hand? Aren't you glad God made your hands so they can do such interesting things? The Bible says . . ." Or, "God made many things for us to enjoy. What can you draw to show something you are thankful for?"

SAND PAINTING

Purpose: That the child share knowledge and understanding of Bible events as well as feelings about them while expressing himself/herself, using the medium.

Materials
☐ Powdered tempera paint
☐ Sand
☐ Cardboard (cut to the desired size for the painting)
☐ Paint containers with lids
☐ Brushes
☐ White glue
☐ Large plastic container to use to mix the sand and paint
☐ Water, paper towels, and sponges for cleanup
☐ Newsprint or old newspapers to cover table

Procedure
1. Place a handful of sand in a large plastic container. The container needs to be large enough for mixing without spilling!
2. Dip a wet brush into dry powdered tempera.
3. With the wet brush, stir the sand until it soaks up the paint and becomes colored. Add more paint until the desired color is obtained.
4. This preparation needs to be completed on the week before it is needed or sometime between class periods to allow it to dry. Speed up the drying process by laying it out on newspaper or in a shallow pan.
5. Plan the design or drawing on cardboard. Sketch lightly with pencil.
6. Apply a layer of white glue to a portion of the drawing. Sprinkle dry sand over the glue area. Shake off the sand that does not stick. It may be used again.
7. Repeat number 6 until the picture or design is complete.

Variations
1. Use sawdust instead of sand. Follow the same procedure.
2. Sand or sawdust painting is effective for map making for older children.

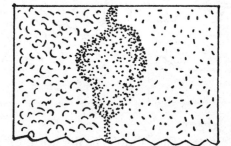

Guided Conversation Ideas
"Show the place on the map where Jesus was when He talked to a large crowd of people." "Which part of your picture shows something that God created?" "How do you feel when this happens to you?"

TEMPERA PAINTING

Purpose: That the child express understandings of Bible events, feelings, or ideas for daily living as he/she paints.

Materials
☐ Tempera (powdered or liquid)
☐ Liquid detergent—to thin liquid tempera as needed
☐ Liquid starch or detergent—to mix powdered tempera
☐ 8 oz. (240 ml) plastic containers with tight-fitting lids. (Other sizes may be used, but 8 oz. is a good amount of paint to mix and store.)
☐ Paint brushes: ½- to 1-inch (1.25-2.5 cm)
☐ Newspapers or plastic drop cloths to cover table and floor
☐ Water, paper towels, and sponges for cleanup
☐ Paint apron or old shirts for painters to wear

Procedure
1. Mix paint in plastic containers. Cover with tight-fitting lids for effective storage between class periods.
2. Provide a brush for each color.
3. Children can paint pictures of Bible events, ways to obey Bible verses, or designs to show God's use of color and/or patterns.
4. Clip paintings to a clothesline or lay in an out-of-the-way place to dry.

Variations
1. Painting may be done on a tabletop, on the floor, on a commercial stand-up easel, or on a pegboard tabletop easel.
2. Paintings can be mounted on a length of butcher paper or shelf paper to make a frieze.
3. Paintings may be bound together in a book for the book table.
4. Children may write or dictate sentences or stories about their paintings.
5. Pictures may be displayed on bulletin boards or hallway walls.

Guided Conversation Ideas
"Tell about your picture." "How did the people feel when Jesus fed them from a small boy's lunch?" "Name the things in your picture that were created by God." "Let's put all of these pictures in order to tell our Bible story. What happened first? What happened next?"

BLOW PAINTING

Purpose: That the child participate in an art activity that will result in a pleasing design that can be used for book covers or simple gifts given as an expression of love and caring.

Materials
- ☐ White or pastel-colored drawing or construction paper
- ☐ Squeeze bottle with tempera paint (liquid or powdered mixed with liquid detergent)
- ☐ Plastic or paper drinking straws
- ☐ Newsprint or old newspapers to cover table
- ☐ Water, paper towels, and sponges for cleanup

Procedure
1. Cover table with newspapers.
2. Place drawing or construction paper on the newspapers.
3. Squeeze little pools of paint onto the paper. A small amount of paint is sufficient.
4. Point one end of the straw in the direction you want the paint to move.
5. BLOW! The straw should not touch the paint.

Variations
1. Use more than one color paint. As the colors meet and mix and form new colors, the child will enjoy talking about the newly-formed color.
2. If younger children are blowing, use food coloring. If blowing becomes sucking, the food coloring is a pleasant alternative to paint.
3. The designs may be used as backing for paintings, bookmarks for gifts, or book covers.

Guided Conversation Ideas
The blowing action will encourage children to explore ideas concerning God's wind. "How do you think the wind felt during the storm? How was it different from a gently blowing wind? Let's look outside. We cannot see the wind. What can you see that tells you the wind is moving? Listen to the wind. Tell about what you hear. "How has God used colors to create a beautiful world?" Look or walk outside. Locate colors that are blended as the blown colors blend.

STRING PAINTING

Purpose: That the child participate in an art activity that will result in a pleasing design that can be used for book or notebook covers or can be framed for a gift.

Materials
☐ Tempera paint
☐ Drawing paper
☐ Shallow pan
☐ String
☐ Newsprint or old newspapers to cover table
☐ Water, paper towels, and sponges for cleanup

Procedure
1. Place tempera paint in a shallow pan.
2. Cover table with old newspapers.
3. Dip one end of the string into the paint. Squeeze out excess paint between sides of the pan and a brush or paper towel.
4. Place the wet part of the string on the paper. Move it back and forth to form a pattern.

Variations
1. Follow the first three steps as above. Place the string in any shape on the paper. Place another piece of paper on the top and hold it in place with one hand. Pull the string sharply with the other hand, moving it in different directions as you pull it out.
2. Make interesting patterns by repeating with different strings and several colors.
3. Use the patterns for backgrounds in the worship center or for book or notebook covers.

Guided Conversation Ideas
"What would you like to do with your pattern? It could be used to wrap a gift. It can be framed and used for a decorative hanging. How can you use it to show love to a friend or someone in your family?"

25

SPATTER PAINTING

Purpose: That children explore an interesting way to produce pictures of items of creation.

Materials
- ☐ Thin tempera paint or shoe polish
- ☐ Toothbrush, vegetable brush, or window-cleaner spray bottle
- ☐ Construction paper (medium to dark colors)
- ☐ Newsprint or old newspaper to cover table
- ☐ Water, paper towels, and sponges for cleanup
- ☐ 15 × 15-inch (37.5 × 37.5 cm) wooden frame with screen attached to the top
- ☐ Items to be painted (leaves, grasses, designs or shapes which have been cut and made ready to place on the construction paper)

Procedure
1. Cover the table with old newspapers or newsprint.
2. Lay the construction paper in place. Medium to dark colors are more effective than pastels.
3. Lay the objects to be painted on the construction paper.
4. Place the thin tempera or shoe polish in a spray bottle.
5. Spray the construction paper.
6. Remove the objects. A soft outline remains.

Variations
1. Occasionally, it will be necessary to pin the items in place.
2. If a screen frame is used, dip a toothbrush or vegetable brush into the thin paint or shoe polish and stroke it across the screen. Remove the screen and the objects that were painted. A soft outline remains.

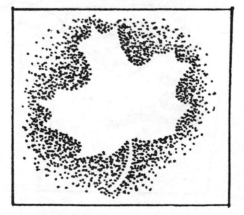

Guided Conversation Ideas
As children select objects to include in their painting, ask, "How did God plan for _____ to be a part of our lives? Can you think of a way to use _____ to help a friend? Tell us about it."

SPONGE PAINTING

Purpose: That the child express ideas and feelings and share information about a Bible event or application of Bible truth.

Materials
- ☐ Powdered or liquid tempera paint
- ☐ Liquid starch or liquid detergent (optional)
- ☐ Paper (butcher or shelf paper works well)
- ☐ Newsprint or old newspaper to cover table
- ☐ Sponges
- ☐ Water, paper towels, and sponges for cleanup
- ☐ Clothespins (optional)
- ☐ Sturdy scissors (optional)
- ☐ Shallow pan

Procedure
1. If powdered paint is used, mix it with water, liquid starch, or liquid detergent. It needs to be the consistency of gravy.
2. Cut sponges into about 1x2-inch (2.5x5 cm) pieces.
3. Place paint in shallow pan.
4. Cover table with newspapers.
5. Clothespins may be clipped to one end of the sponge. If the child holds the clothespin while working with the paint, very little paint will be on his/her hands.
6. Dip end of sponge into paint. Pick up only a little paint.
7. Tap paint end of sponge on the area of paper to be covered.

Variations
1. Sponges may be cut into simple shapes and stamped onto the paper to form a picture or design.
2. Older children may enjoy using sponge painting to make notebook or folder covers.

Guided Conversation Ideas
As children sponge paint light, spring grass, sky, and trees, talk about the marvelous beauty of God's creation. Look outside to see some of the beauty. "God is so good to give us eyes to see how He has created a beautiful world!"

GADGET PRINTING

Purpose: That children use a variety of objects to make patterns and designs with paint.

Materials
☐ Powdered or liquid tempera paint
☐ Liquid starch or detergent to mix paint if powdered tempera is used
☐ Shallow pan
☐ Construction paper
☐ Transparent adhesive paper (optional)
☐ Gadgets such as cookie cutters, potato masher, spools, cork, etc.
☐ Newsprint or old newspapers to cover table
☐ Water, paper towels, and sponges for cleanup

Procedure
1. Mix and pour paint into the shallow pan. Tempera needs to be the consistency of thick gravy.
2. Fold a paper towel and place it into the tempera, forming a stamp pad.
3. Place the "gadget" on the stamp pad and stamp the design onto the construction paper.

Variations
1. Older children will enjoy stamping designs and patterns on burlap or muslin to make banners.
2. Cover the designed paper with transparent adhesive paper. The finished product may be used for a place mat or it may be cut into strips to be used for bookmarks. A group may wish to make a large number of bookmarks to be used for gifts for a hospital or home for the elderly.
3. Bible verses may be lettered on the paper before it is covered.

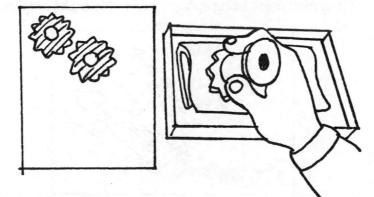

Guided Conversation Ideas
When teaching John 15:12 (NIV), "My command is this: Love each other as I have loved you," plan for specific ways to show love by preparing simple gifts of bookmarks or place mats.

VEGETABLE PRINTING

Purpose: That child:
- plan ways to use vegetables and paint to make a pattern.
- use the finished product in a way to show love to a friend or family member.

Materials
☐ Powdered or liquid tempera
☐ Liquid starch or detergent to mix paint if powdered tempera is used
☐ Shallow pan
☐ Construction paper
☐ Transparent adhesive paper (optional)
☐ Potatoes (other vegetables may be used, if desired)
☐ Newsprint or old newspapers to cover table
☐ Water, paper towels, and sponges for cleanup

Procedure
1. Mix powdered tempera with starch or detergent and place it in the shallow pan. Pour liquid tempera into the pan. Tempera should be the consistency of gravy.
2. Fold a paper towel and place it into the tempera, forming a stamp pad.
3. Cut the potato in half. Carve the design or shape to be stamped on the cut side.
4. Place the stamp on the paint pad to pick up paint, and stamp it onto the paper. A variety of stamps may be cut, and pleasing patterns made, as they are stamped in patterns on the paper.

Variations
1. Pleasing patterns may be made by using the shape of several kinds of vegetables without carving a design. The crosswise shape of a green pepper, the end of a celery rib, the rings of an onion that has been sliced across are a few of the possibilities.
2. Consider stamping on a large piece of construction paper. Cover both sides of the paper with transparent adhesive paper. This will make a durable place mat. One mat may be made for each member of the child's family for gifts.
3. Bible verse may be lettered on the paper before it is covered.

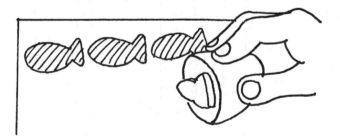

Guided Conversation Ideas
Read Genesis 1:11. "God thought of many kinds of plants to give us food." You may want to bring extra pieces of vegetables being used so children can taste them.

BLOCK PRINTING

Purpose: That children may create patterns and designs related to their Bible study as they make and/or use block prints.

Materials
- ☐ Bibles
- ☐ Paint or ink
- ☐ Wooden blocks
- ☐ Construction paper or other surface to be printed
- ☐ Knife to cut stamp into wood
- ☐ Water, paper towels, and sponges for cleanup
- ☐ Newspaper to cover work area
- ☐ Shallow pans for paint

Procedure
1. Older children may cut their own design, shape, or object in the wood. The blocks need to be cut before class time for younger children.
2. If paint is used, make a stamp pad by placing layers of paper towels or a sponge in a shallow pan of paint. The stamp can be pressed onto the stamp pad and then printed onto the paper surface.

Variations
1. Use potatoes or other vegetables to make the print.
2. Finished prints may be used for the background in the worship area.
3. Use the prints for notebook covers or Bible or hymnbook covers.
4. Prints may be stamped onto tissue paper and used for wrapping paper at a gift giving time.
5. Use simple designs that are in some way related to the Bible story or the Bible verse, or that will be used in some kind of service project.

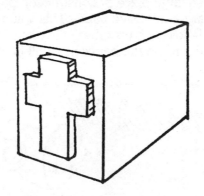

Guided Conversation Ideas
"How do you think _____ will feel when he/she opens the gift that you have wrapped in this paper?" "What does a gift tell the person who receives it?" "How does the pattern you have made help us to think about _____?"

MELTED CRAYONS

Purpose: That children use an unusual medium when expressing understandings, feelings, and ideas.

Materials
☐ Old crayon stubs (with paper covering removed)
☐ Shelf paper or drawing paper
☐ Wax paper
☐ Shaving tool (grater, dull vegetable peeler)
☐ Iron
☐ Muffin tins or egg cartons

Procedure
1. Grate or shave crayon stubs. Use muffin tins or egg cartons for storage, placing a different color in each section.
2. Sprinkle some crayon chips on a piece of shelf paper or drawing paper.
3. Place a second sheet on top of the crayon chips.
4. Use a warm iron to press on this second paper and melt the crayons. The iron needs only to be warm—not hot enough to burn hands and/or fingers.
5. Remove the top paper and draw with a black crayon over the melted colors or use scissors to scratch a design or picture into the wax.

Variations
1. Use wax paper instead of shelf paper. The resulting hanging will be quite effective when it is hung in a window and the light shines through.
2. Bible pictures and/or verses may be placed between the pieces of wax paper before ironing it. Pieces will stay in place.
3. Iron back and forth if you desire the crayons to melt together smoothly. Lift the iron as you move it to obtain a spotty effect.
4. Melt crayons in muffin cups and use the wax as liquid paint. Use cotton swabs or craft sticks to apply the melted crayons. Be sure to line the muffin tin with paper cup cake liners for easy cleanup.
5. Melt stubs of crayons together in paper-lined muffin cups. Place different colors in the same cup for variety. Allow the melted wax to harden. Cool and peel off paper liners. The resulting crayon will be a good shape and size for younger children to use.

Guided Conversation Ideas
"God plans for us to care for His world. He is pleased when we use materials carefully. Let's use old crayons in a special way that is fun and that uses something that is often thrown away."

CRAYON RUBBINGS

Purpose: That the child use a textured crayon technique to illustrate Bible events or feelings or ideas.

Materials

- ☐ Newsprint, ditto paper, or typing paper (two sheets for each rubbing)
- ☐ Crayons (paper removed so that the broad side can be used)
- ☐ Paper clips (four to be used for each rubbing)
- ☐ Textured items to be rubbed (leaves, tree bark, screen, fishnet, etc.)

Procedure

1. Place the items to be rubbed on one of the pieces of paper.
2. Lay the second sheet on top of the items.
3. Paper clip the papers together at each side.
4. Use the broad side of the crayon(s) to rub over the top sheet of paper. The result will be a shadowy picture of the items.

Variations

1. Use lightweight cardboard to cut out shapes to be rubbed. Use shapes to make patterns and designs. Cut out Bible story figures, placing them on the paper in such a way as to tell the Bible story. The resulting rub will review and reinforce the Bible story.
2. Use corrugated paper (or cardboard) for interesting effects.
3. Mix and overlap a variety of colors.
4. Pictures may be framed and/or mounted and used on bulletin boards or walls of the classroom.

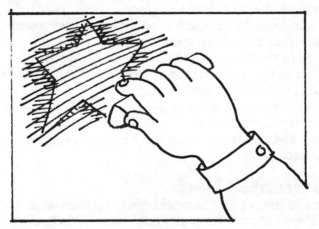

Guided Conversation Ideas

When objects from nature are used, read Genese 1:11 and ask, "What does the bark tell you about creation? Tell about the different kinds of leaves." When placing cutout Bible story shapes in place, ask the children to tell the story. Talk about what happened next and next in order to reinforce sequence.

CRAYON ETCHINGS

Purpose: That the children express their understanding of a Bible verse/story as they work with an interesting way to use crayons.

Materials
☐ Crayons (a good supply of black)
☐ Drawing paper or white construction paper
☐ Bibles
☐ A "scratching tool" such as edge of spoon, scissors, nail, bent paper clip
☐ Newsprint or newspaper to cover the work area

Procedure
1. Cover the paper with one or many colors of crayons. Color heavily to leave a thick layer of crayon. If more than one color is used, the resulting "etching" will be more interesting than if only one color is used.
2. Completely cover this with black crayon.
3. While the layers of color are being added, talk about the Bible verse (or story) that is going to be etched. Read it from the Bible. "What does this verse say that we need to do?" "How will it help us to get along well at school?" The verse may be repeated and memorized.
4. Scratch through the black with tool to make design, picture, or Bible verse. Scratch through other layers as desired to reveal a variety of color.

Variations
1. The Bible verse mottos may be hung on the wall or bulletin board.
2. The pictures may be wrapped and used for gifts.
3. The crayon colors may be covered with black or violet paint that has been mixed with liquid detergent. Draw with the tools.

Guided Conversation Ideas
"How will this Bible verse help you to get along well with your brother or sister? Can you tell us another verse that teaches us the same thing?" "Find all the words in the verse that are verbs. What action will you take?" "Who wrote the book in the Bible that contains this verse? To whom was it written?"

CRAYON RESIST

Purpose: That the child share the Bible story by making pictures to show the sequence of events.

Materials
- [ ] Crayons
- [ ] Drawing paper or construction paper
- [ ] Water colors or thin tempera paint
- [ ] Paint brushes
- [ ] Water, paper towels, and sponges for cleanup
- [ ] Newsprint or newspapers to cover the table
- [ ] An area to be used for drying the paintings

Procedure
1. Talk about the Bible story. Decide which part of the story the child will draw. A small group can work together, each drawing a different part of the story.
2. Make the picture with crayons, pressing firmly.
3. Brush lightly over the entire paper with thin paint. Best results are obtained when one color is used. The paint will not adhere to the wax of the crayon and the picture will be visible through the paint. Place the picture in your drying area.

Variations
1. Place wax paper over a white piece of paper. Draw on it with a pencil. Press hard enough to transfer the wax to the white drawing paper. Brush the paint over the wax lines on the white paper and watch the words or pictures appear.
2. Write Bible verses with a white crayon on white drawing paper. Wash over the words with thin paint and watch the verse appear. One child may wish to write the verse and give it to another to discover.
3. Surprise pictures or verses may be made to send to a child who is sick. Give directions to wash over the picture to watch the surprise appear.

Guided Conversation Ideas
Read Bible stories and verses as the children work. "What part of the Bible story will you show?" "What happened next?" "How did the man feel?" "If you had been there, how would you have felt?" "What will you do this week to obey the verse that you are writing?"

COAT OF ARMS

Purpose: That the child review and share information about a Bible person as he/she designs a coat of arms for that person.

Materials
☐ Bibles
☐ Lightweight poster board, drawing paper, or butcher paper
☐ Pencils, felt pens, or crayons
☐ Scissors (optional)

Procedure
1. Read and talk about the Bible person that has been selected for the coat of arms project.
2. Draw a shield on a piece of paper.
3. Divide the shield into four sections.
4. Draw in each of the four sections a symbol that will show a significant fact about the Bible person.
5. Shields may be displayed on bulletin boards or wall areas.

Variations
1. Make a shield for each of the 12 disciples. Write the disciples' names on small index cards. Match the cards to the shields.
2. Work in pairs or teams with one person/team asking questions about the Bible person and the other person/team answering the question with an appropriate drawing in one section of the shield.
3. Make a personal or family shield.

Guided Conversation Ideas
"What can you draw that will show how Joseph's brothers felt about him?" "In the next section of the shield, draw something to show how the brothers tricked their father." "What can you draw in the third section to show something that happened to Joseph in Egypt?" "Tell us about the meeting between Joseph and his brothers." "In the last section of the shield, draw something that will tell about that meeting."

POSTERS

Purpose: That the child share an idea in a simple form so that it can be understood at a glance.

Materials
☐ Poster board
☐ Felt pens
☐ Cutout letter patterns and construction paper
☐ Newspapers and/or magazines (for word posters)
☐ Scissors
☐ Glue

Procedure
1. Decide on the one idea that the poster will communicate.
2. Plan for a simple illustration and clear lettering.
3. Use cutout letters or felt pens to letter the poster.
4. The illustration may be drawn, painted, or cut out and pasted onto the poster board.
5. More than one poster may be needed to accomplish the goals of the activity.
6. Display posters on bulletin boards or walls.

Variations
1. Posters may be made to publicize upcoming activities such as a class project, a party, an outing, or VBS.
2. Word posters may be made using a collection of words cut or torn from magazines or newspapers. The words should be glued onto poster board in a shape which communicates the idea of the poster. Example: A question may be put on a question mark shape.
3. Encourage child to imagine that he/she is a Bible person. Make the poster to show an idea that the Bible person might share.

Guided Conversation Ideas
"What idea do you want your poster to communicate?" "What are some words that will help to communicate this idea?" "What idea could Noah share on a poster that he would put in the area where he was building the ark?" "What idea about his missionary journey could Paul share on a travel poster?"

MURAL

Purpose: That a small group of children experience the learning that occurs from planning and working together to express ideas, feelings, and understandings as a group rather than individually.

Materials
- [ ] Bibles
- [ ] Length of butcher paper or shelf paper—usually 6 or 8 feet by 2 or 3 feet (1.8 or 2.4 m by 60 or 90 cm)—depending on your group size and working area
- [ ] Brushes or sponges
- [ ] Tempera paint (liquid or powdered to be mixed with liquid detergent)
- [ ] Newsprint, old newspaper, or plastic drop cloths to cover area
- [ ] Water, paper towels, and sponges for cleanup
- [ ] Aprons or old shirts to cover painters

Procedure
1. Plan together what the mural will show. List ideas on chalkboard or chart.
2. Check Scripture to clarify ideas, understandings, and sequence of events.
3. Decide which person in the group will be responsible for each part. Record responsibilities on chalkboard or chart.
4. Simple pencil sketching will help to define areas.
5. Paint mural.

Variations
1. Background may be sponge painted or finger painted.
2. Objects may be cut or torn out of construction paper and attached to the background while the paint is still wet. Paint will act as adhesive as it dries.
3. Use broad side of crayon stubs (without paper covering) for backgrounds.
4. Felt pens, crayons, or water color paints may be used.
5. Possibilities for murals are unlimited! Encourage imaginative thinking.

Guided Conversation Ideas
The decision-making process is a valuable part of mural-making! Encourage children to explore alternatives by asking, "What is another way to do it? Which way will be best for us today? How can more than one person work at the same time? What does our Bible verse say? How will that help us work together now and also at home or at school?"

FRIEZE

Purpose: That the children arrange in sequence the events of the Bible story.

Materials
☐ Long strip of shelf paper, newsprint, or butcher paper for the background
☐ Glue
☐ Pencils, crayons, or felt pens
☐ Bibles
☐ Bible story visual aids (optional)
☐ Drawing paper or construction paper
☐ Scissors (optional)

Procedure
1. Read the Bible story. List the events on a chalkboard or chart paper.
2. Select the events that will be illustrated.
3. Decide which child will do which picture.
4. Give directions for using whatever materials you have available.
5. Make the pictures. While children are drawing, ask questions about the sequence of events; for example, "What happened after Jesus entered Jerusalem on a donkey?" "Where did Jesus go after the Last Supper?"
6. When the pictures have been completed, place them in sequence on the background paper. Check to see that they are in the correct order.
7. Glue them in place.
8. Put on the wall or bulletin board or perhaps out on the hall wall.

Variations
1. Tear or cut out some of the figures for the pictures.
2. Make a taped narration to explain what is happening in each picture.
3. Plan for children to tell about their picture. Some may wish to read the Bible verse that the picture is about.

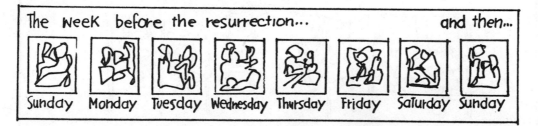

Guided Conversation Ideas
A study of Holy Week lends itself to making a frieze. A child or pair of children might work on each day of the week. Pictures of events for each day are completed and placed in sequence. "What did the disciples think about Jesus washing their feet?" "What did Judas do on Tuesday?" "What happened in the Garden of Gethsemane?" "How would you feel if one of your friends betrayed you?"

CARTOONING

Purpose: That children express their feelings and think about application of Bible truth as they draw and talk about real-life situations.

Materials
☐ Bibles
☐ Pencils, crayons, or felt pens
☐ Paper (shelf paper cut into 6 × 36-inch [15 × 90 cm] pieces works well)
☐ Chalkboard and chalk or chart paper and pens

Procedure
1. Read and talk about the Bible verses that are being studied. Ask questions to help children decide what they want to show in their cartoons. (See "Guided Conversation Ideas.")
2. Divide the paper into squares. For younger children, do this before class time.
3. Encourage children to list the sequence of events they wish to show. It will help to list them on the chalkboard or chart paper.
4. Children will enjoy drawing simple pictures without too much detail.
5. Conversation may be included in "balloons."

Variations
1. Cartoons may be displayed on bulletin board or wall.
2. They may be duplicated as part of a newspaper and distributed to class members. If they are used for this purpose, they will need to be smaller to fit the newspaper format.
3. Cartoons are an effective means for children to use in depicting a real-life situation. For example, children use the first few squares to show the situation or problem and the last few squares to show what the cartoon people will do if they obey God's command.

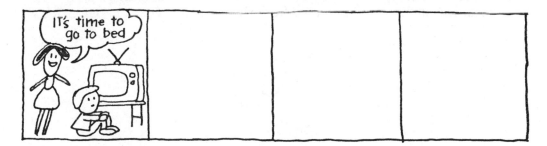

Guided Conversation Ideas
"What are some ways you can obey God's direction to be a good friend when a new child comes to your room at school?" "What would be a good thing to do when your brother or sister bothers something that is in your room?" "What happens when Mother or Dad ask you to do something that you really do not want to do?"

MOBILES

Purpose: That the child share events from a Bible story, feelings about a Bible verse, or application of Scripture as he/she makes a mobile (a dimensional design that hangs in space and moves with the air).

Materials
- ☐ Hangers or small wooden dowels to use for crosspieces
- ☐ Nylon thread, fishing line, or string
- ☐ Construction paper
- ☐ Scissors
- ☐ Water, paper towels, and sponges as needed for cleanup

Procedure
1. Plan with the child. Help him/her decide what to show in the mobile. Children may work in pairs or small groups to complete one mobile.
2. Decide how to make the pictures or other parts that will go on the mobile.
3. When pictures/parts are completed, tie them to crosspiece(s). Let younger children use one crosspiece such as a hanger or piece of dowel. Older children may use several crosspieces. Learning occurs, and children are pleased with their work, even if the mobile does not balance perfectly. The mobile should be assembled from the bottom up in order to keep it balanced.
4. Hang the mobile in a place where the air is moving. Place it as near the eye level of the children as possible.

Variations
1. Starched string designs may be made by soaking soft string or yarn in starch or white glue. Place the wet string on wax paper spread over cardboard or layers of newspaper. Pin or tie the ends together to be sure the yarn holds its shape. When it is dry, paint it with tempera and shellac it. Or leave it as it is.
2. Small pictures or lightweight objects may be used on a mobile.
3. Objects and shapes can be formed from chenille wire.

Guided Conversation Ideas
"How do the pictures on the mobile show ways the people and the missionaries in _____ work together? Why is this important?" "Do you think _____ would like to have this mobile at home to be reminded about the Bible story even though he is sick?" "Name one other picture or thing you can put on the mobile to tell one other part of the story."

PAPER TEARING AND CUTTING

Purpose: That the children use a torn- or cut-paper technique to demonstrate their feelings and/or understandings about a Bible passage/story.

Materials
- ☐ Construction paper (assorted colors and sizes)
- ☐ Background paper (optional)
- ☐ Glue (optional)
- ☐ Felt pens or crayons (optional)
- ☐ Scissors

Procedure
1. Plan the shapes needed to share feelings and/or understandings about the selected Bible passage/story. Read Bibles as plans are made.
2. Hold paper firmly between thumb and forefinger. Use the thumb and forefinger of other hand to tear the shape. Tear a small section at a time. Keep the shape simple. Omit fine details.
3. Add a few details with pens or crayons if desired.
4. If the child wishes, the torn or cut items may be glued to a background to be displayed and shared with others.

Variations
1. Tear or cut shapes that are related to memory verses and ask children to match the shape with words in the verse. For example, ask the children to tear or cut shapes of things that God has created. Number seven sheets of paper, each with one of the numerals 1-7. Ask children to place their torn shape on the paper that will show which day that item was created.
2. Simple shapes may be torn or cut and used on a flannelboard to tell the Bible or application story.
3. Shapes may be torn or cut to use for a bulletin board border or for name tags.

Guided Conversation Ideas
Thank God for hands and fingers that can do many things. "What happened first?" "Show us the next thing that happened, etc." "Look around our room and show us something else that is the same shape or the same color." "What things in your picture tell us something that God made?"

TISSUE PAPER AND STARCH

Purpose: That children:
- talk about God's gift of sight as they experiment with color;
- work together to make a background for (1) a Bible story scene or (2) objects and figures which will illustrate ways to obey God's Word.

Materials
- ☐ Starch or white glue diluted with water to creamy consistency
- ☐ Assorted colors, sizes, and shapes of tissue paper
- ☐ Drawing paper or manila paper
- ☐ Shallow pans for starch
- ☐ ½- to 1-inch (1.25-2.5 cm) paint brushes
- ☐ Newsprint or newspapers to cover work area
- ☐ Water, paper towels, and sponges for cleanup
- ☐ Scissors (optional)

Procedure
1. Read Bible verses or Bible story.
2. Talk about/plan what the child wants to share in his tissue paper and starch work.
3. Tear or cut tissue paper into desired sizes and shapes.
4. Pour a small amount of starch or glue into shallow pan.
5. Dip brush into starch or glue. Wipe off excess on side of pan.
6. Place tissue paper onto background paper.
7. Brush over the tissue with the starch. The starch will act as a fixative and the tissue paper will adhere to the drawing paper.

Variations
1. The drawing paper may be entirely covered with tissue paper. The resulting paper may be used as a background for torn or cut paper objects.
2. When different colors of tissue paper are overlapped, new and different colors will be the result.
3. Older children may enjoy using shellac instead of starch. The resulting product will be quite durable.
4. Use white tissue paper for the background and "paint" onto it the colored tissue pieces. Hang the tissue paper "picture" in the window. The light shining through will produce a very pleasing effect.

Guided Conversation Ideas
As colors overlap and blend, talk about God's use of color in the world around us. Plan to walk outside or around the room to locate colors that match those in the tissue paper. Thank God for eyes to see the colors in His world.

STITCHERY

Purpose: That the child design a simple picture or symbol to express feelings and/or understandings about a Bible story or verse.

Materials
- [ ] Bibles
- [ ] Loosely-woven fabric such as burlap
- [ ] Yarn (this is a good way to use up a variety of scraps)
- [ ] Paper and pencils for planning
- [ ] Plastic needles with large eyes (yarn needles)
- [ ] Scissors

Procedure
1. Read and talk about the Bible story/verses.
2. Decide what feelings or ideas the child wishes to show.
3. Sketch a simple plan on paper, then on fabric.
4. Stitch on top of the lines on the fabric.
5. Running stitches and outline stitches are sufficient for most children. Occasionally, a child may wish to use the satin stitch to fill in an area.
6. When child has completed work, it may be displayed as a wall hanging or in the worship center until it is taken home.

Variations
1. Place a dowel stick at the top end of the fabric. Sew a small hem and add a piece of yarn for hanging.
2. Edges may be fringed for a pleasing finish.
3. The stitchery may be mounted on cardboard and framed as a picture.

Guided Conversation Ideas
Talk about ways the symbols chosen share an idea or feeling. For example, "How does the cross remind you of Jesus' love?" "Tell us why you stitched a fish shape." "If the star could talk, what would it say about the birth of Jesus?"

DOUGH

Purpose: That the child:
● experience using a mix-and-squeeze material;
● be involved in a cooperative activity with others.

Materials
☐ Salt
☐ Flour
☐ Water
☐ Cream of tartar
☐ Cooking oil
☐ Measuring cup and spoons
☐ Large plastic mixing bowl
☐ Spoon
☐ Wax paper (optional, depending on the recipe used)
☐ Electric skillet or kettle and stove (optional)
☐ Airtight container or plastic bag

Procedure
1. Mix together 6 cups (1.44 l) flour and 1¾ cups (.42 l)salt.
2. Add 2 cups (.48 l) water slowly, mixing well.
3. Knead on board. Dough may be rolled out and cut or shaped with hands.
4. If desired, this dough may be baked at 225°F (107°C) for one hour. Or dough may dry thoroughly. When finished, paint and shellac.

Variations
1. Add food coloring to the water before mixing. Powdered tempera may be added to the flour to color dough.
2. The sense of smell may be utilized by adding a teaspoon of extract to the liquid—orange, lemon, mint, strawberry, cherry, and others are pleasant additions.
3. For a soft dough that does not harden, but is long-lasting when stored in an airtight container and refrigerated, use the following recipe (play dough). Mix 3 cups (.72 l) flour, 1½ cups (.36 l) salt, 2 tbsp. (30 ml) cooking oil, 6 tbsp. (90 ml) cream of tartar, and 3 cups (.72 l) water. Bring to a boil, cook on high until it pulls away from the pan. Works well in an electric skillet (moderate heat). Remove from heat, drop on wax paper and knead well. Color may be added with the liquid.

Note: If dough sticks to skillet, fill skillet with boiling water to make it easy to clean.

Guided Conversation Ideas
"God made us in a special way. He gave us hands to feel, squeeze, and shape dough. Our eyes can see pretty colors. We can smell good smells!" Talk about colors, fragrances, and textures in relation to creation and/or things that are in the classroom environment.

CLAY

Purpose: That children use clay or dough mixture to model forms that help tell a Bible story or express ideas, feelings, or understandings.

Materials
☐ Plastic drop cloth to cover floor under work area
☐ Newsprint or newspapers to cover table
☐ Wax paper on top of the newspaper in the area that the child will use for the clay or dough
☐ Clay or dough (the kind to use will be dependent on the project)
☐ Tray or box to store finished work
☐ Airtight containers to keep unfinished work damp and ready to work on during the next class period
☐ Water, paper towels, and sponges for cleanup
☐ Paint aprons or discarded shirts to cover children

Procedure
1. Talk with children to decide what they want to model.
2. Purchase clay or make dough to use for the modeling.
3. Prepare the work area: cover the floor and table with newsprint or newspapers. Place wax paper in the area that will be used for the clay or dough.
4. Ask children to wear aprons or old shirts to protect clothing.
5. Knead, pound, and mold the clay or dough into the desired objects.

Variations
1. You may use clay that hardens or a non-hardening dough. The choice depends upon your project.
2. Dough or clay may be used to hold up chenille wire or clothespin people in dioramas.
3. Animals, people, and other objects may be made from clay for use in dioramas and other scenes.
4. Shape bowls, lamps, etc., to demonstrate the kinds of objects that were used by people in Bible times.
5. Simple gift items may be made with clay that hardens. Items may be painted and covered with shellac.
6. Children will enjoy helping you make the dough in preparation for classtime use. See recipes on page 44.

Guided Conversation Ideas
If children are modeling items used by people in Bible times, talk about how each item was used and how it compares to something we use today. Ask about the scenes or dioramas that children are making as they model animals, people, or other items for the scene. "What happened after _____?" "How would you feel if you were the person in the scene?" "How did the people depend upon God?" "In what ways can we depend upon God to help us?"

PAPIER-MACHÉ

Purpose: That older children make puppets and/or maps, using papier-maché for their modeling material.

Materials
- ☐ Balloons (for puppet base)
- ☐ Cardboard (for map base)
- ☐ Salad oil
- ☐ Starch (liquid)
- ☐ Paper towels or newspapers
- ☐ Water, paper towels, and sponges for cleanup
- ☐ Newsprint or newspapers to cover work area

Procedure
1. Cover the table and surrounding floor area. The starch will drip!
2. If you desire to make puppet heads, blow up the balloons. Cover each one with salad oil.
3. Dip the torn strips of paper towels or newspapers in a shallow pan of liquid starch. Pull the paper between second and third fingers to remove excess starch.
4. Place the strips over and around the balloon.
5. Allow this to dry. Another layer may be applied if desired. When papier-maché is dry, remove the balloon.
6. If the papier-maché is being used in the making of maps, use it to show the mountains and hilly parts of the country.
7. When completed project is dry, paint it with tempera paints or poster paints.
8. Puppets, objects, or maps may be shellacked.

Variations
1. Facial tissues and spray starch may be used on balloon bases.
2. Wheat paste may be mixed with newspaper instead of using starch.

Guided Conversation Ideas
"How will your puppet help to tell the Bible story? What are some things you will want it to say?" "Imagine that your puppet is _____. What will it say? What would it do? How would that be obeying God's Word?" "On your map, label the places where Jesus was when _____."

ART ACTIVITIES

DIORAMA

Purpose: That the child create a scene from the Bible story or a scene that will illustrate the application in his life of the story or a Bible verse.

Materials
- [ ] Bibles
- [ ] Boxes (shoe boxes are a good size and shape)
- [ ] Scissors
- [ ] Glue
- [ ] Crayons, felt pens, or paint
- [ ] Scraps of fabric or crepe paper to make clothes for figures
- [ ] Pipe cleaners or round-top clothespins
- [ ] Clay or dough in which to stand the figures

Procedure
1. Read Bible to review subject matter for the scenes.
2. Plan what will be included in the scene and who will do which part.
3. If it is an inside scene, the sides of the box can be the walls. If the scene is outdoors, background of sky, ground, etc., may be drawn or painted inside the box.
4. Prepare the people, animals, or other parts of the scene.
5. Use clay or dough to stand the figures in the box.

Variations
1. Children may work in pairs or small groups to make one scene.
2. Larger scenes may be made if corrugated boxes are used. Select the size that is appropriate for your purpose. Cut away the top and proceed as with the shoe boxes.
3. Scenes may be placed in window sills or on counters or tables to be viewed by others in the class or they may be taken to other classes to be shared.

Guided Conversation Ideas
"Tell three things the people in your scene are doing. What did Jesus say about that?" "When do you need to make a decision like _____?" "How do you feel when that happens?" "Name another Bible story/verse that teaches us the same thing."

TV BOX

Purpose: That the child express his/her ideas, feelings, and knowledge about a Bible event or about the relationship of the Bible study to his/her life.

Materials
☐ Cardboard box
☐ Knife or scissors for cutting viewing hole in side of box (opening to resemble TV screen)
☐ Rollers—broomstick pieces or dowel sticks ½ to 1 inch (1.25-2.5 cm) long
☐ Long strip of shelf paper or butcher paper to attach to the rollers
☐ Paper for drawings—newsprint, manila, or drawing
☐ Tempera, water colors, crayons, or felt markers
☐ Glue—to fasten pictures in sequence to strip of paper
☐ Tape or glue to fasten strip of paper to rollers
☐ Sponges, water, paper towels as needed for cleanup

Procedure
1. Cut the screen-shape out of one side of a cardboard box.
2. Cut holes in top and bottom of box to fit rollers.
3. Prepare length of shelf paper or butcher paper to fit rollers.
4. Help children think about and decide what they want to show in their pictures.
5. Children draw or paint pictures to illustrate events and ideas.
6. Mount pictures on the strip of paper.
7. Attach strip of paper to rollers.
8. Turn the rollers from one side to the other to show the pictures.

Variations
1. Children may make individual TV sets by using a paper bag. Cut the opening in one side of the bag. Make a slit on each side of the opening. Cut shelf paper to a size that will slide through. Draw pictures onto the strip and insert through the slits.
2. A taped narration may be prepared to accompany the showing of the pictures. Provide tape recorder and blank cassette tape.

Guided Conversation Ideas
Identify the most important parts of the story in order to decide what to include.
"Which thing happened next? How would you feel if you were _____?"
"Make three pictures to show how you would obey Ephesians 6:1."

DRAMA ACTIVITIES

Combine a child's imagination, feelings and actions in dramatic activities and the end result can be a very effective learning experience.

Benefits
- Dramatic activities provide a unique opportunity to briefly step into another person's shoes, and experience for the moment some of his/her attitudes and feelings.
- Roleplaying and open-ended situations help children relate Bible truths to present-day experiences.
- Acting out specific examples of loving, sharing, kindness, friendliness, caring and helping gives concrete meaning to these otherwise abstract words.

Tips
1. Dramatic activities do not require that children write or follow a script. Rather, children's words and actions grow out of having heard their teacher tell a story or recount a particular situation.
2. Provide a dress-up box of fabric and simple props to help stimulate children's thinking.
3. Also use pictures to provide children with information about customs and clothing. Plan for an area in the room that can be cleared of furnishings and used as a stage for the dramatization.
4. If children feel unsure of themselves, they will sometimes try to cover up their insecurity by acting silly. To prevent this:
   - Start with very simple stories/situations.
   - Talk over the story/situation in enough detail so children feel sure of what to do.
   - Demonstrate how a specific part or action might be acted out or pantomimed (or let a volunteer do this). Then let several children show how they would do it.
   - If a child pauses during the drama, ask a question to help him/her remember the action of the story or think of what to do next.
   - Don't force a child to act out a story or situation, but do involve him/her in other ways: planning, evaluating, prop-making, etc.
5. If some children are shy, encourage their participation by suggesting non-threatening parts they might take (parts with little or no speaking). Praise them for the good job they did. As they feel success in small parts, their confidence will grow and they will often volunteer for more involved parts.
6. Remember that the value of drama activities is in the *process*, not necessarily in putting on a *performance*.

PLAY THE STORY

Purpose: That children:
- show/reinforce their understanding of what happened in a Bible event;
- portray the feelings of Bible characters in preparation for discussing (1) their own feelings in a similar situation; (2) ways to live out a Bible truth in this type of situation.

Materials
Children can act out stories without any costumes, props or scenery, but these items often stimulate their interest and add to their enjoyment (see "Variations" below). Use as time permits.

Procedure
1. Tell the story, using conversation as well as description.
2. Review the story with the group. Guide them to think through the story and sequence of events by asking questions:
   a. What happened first in the story?
   b. Who were the people? What did they say?
   c. How do you think they felt? How can you show this?
   d. What happened next in the story?
   e. Discuss each scene, its time period and location.
3. Guide children to identify the story characters as you list them on a chart. Decide who will play each character. If several children wish to play the same part, play story several times, taking turns.
4. Act out the story. If a child pauses, ask a question to help him/her remember the action of the story.
5. Guide the children to evaluate the results by asking questions such as, "What did you like best about the way the story was acted out?" "What are some ways we might change what we said or did?"
6. Act out the story again.

Variations
1. Let children use costumes and props in acting out the story.
2. Let children make scenery to use in the story. Supply shelf paper, poster board, felt pens, paint, brushes, scissors, glue, tape.

Guided Conversation
After playing the story, ask questions to help children relate the Bible truth to everyday living. For example, after children act out the story of Daniel and his friends refusing the king's food, ask questions such as, "How do you think Daniel and his friends felt when they were commanded to do something they knew God did not want them to do?" "Think about some times when someone tried to get you to do something God does not want you to do. How did you feel? What can you do when you need courage to do right?"

PANTOMIME

Purpose: That children use actions without words to convey:
- the feelings of Bible characters;
- the sequence of Bible events;
- ways to apply Bible verses to daily living;
- the meaning of a song.

Materials

No materials are needed.

Procedure

Follow procedure for "Play the Story" (page 50), except that children do not speak as they act out the story. They convey the entire story through their actions. Give special emphasis to the feelings of Bible characters and how to express them.

Variations

1. Let children pantomime ways to obey Bible commands. Children enjoy pantomiming and letting the rest of the group guess what they are doing. Example: Children act out ways to obey God's command "Children, obey your parents" (Ephesians 6:1). If the group has trouble guessing what the child is doing, they may ask questions that can be answered yes or no, such as, "Are you inside the house? Are you in the kitchen?"
2. Many children's songs lend themselves to pantomime. A child may show through pantomime the way the music makes him feel; for example, happy, sad, etc. He may show the action indicated by the words of the song or the meaning of the song as he understands it.

Guided Conversation Ideas

Here are two ways to get children started using pantomime.

1. "I'm going to act out a way I can obey this Bible verse, but I'm not going to use any words. See if you can guess what I'm doing." After children guess what you are doing, say, "Who would like to act out another way to obey this verse and let us guess what you are doing?"
2. Prepare index cards that suggest ways to obey a Bible verse; for example, "Make your bed." "Rake the leaves." Say, "These cards tell some ways to obey God's command to obey your parents. Take a card. Read what it says, but don't show it to anyone. Then act out what your card says—but don't use any words. See if we can guess what you are doing." When children are comfortable with acting out ideas given to them, include some cards that say, "Think of a way to obey this verse (quote verse). Act it out, but don't use any words." Or you can eliminate the use of cards at this point.

PUPPETS—Bible Times

Purpose: That children use puppets to:
- show/reinforce their understanding of what happened in a Bible event;
- portray the feelings of Bible characters in preparation for discussing (1) their own feelings in a similar situation; (2) ways to live out a Bible truth in this type of situation.

Materials
☐ Bible times puppets (children can make their own or use puppets from Puppet Box)—see pages 54-56.
☐ Stage (optional)—see page 56.

Procedure
Follow the steps outlined for "Play the Story," page 50. Children who have difficulty expressing their feelings will be better able to put feelings into words and actions when using a simple puppet.

Variations
A puppet play can be presented with or without a script. A puppet script can be written either by the teacher or students.

Guided Conversation
After playing the story, ask questions to help children relate the Bible truth to everyday living. For example, after children act out the story of Joseph's jealous brothers, ask questions such as, "What made Joseph's brothers feel jealous? What did they do because they were jealous? Everyone feels jealous at some time or other—either because of wanting something someone else has or wanting to be able to do something someone else can do. Think about a time when *you* have felt jealous of someone—when you have wanted something someone else had—or when you wanted to be able to do something someone else could do. What do you want to do to a person if you feel jealous? Romans 12:15 tells us what God wants us to do when someone is happy about something. Why is this sometimes hard to do? What can you do when you find it hard to be happy with someone who has received something you wish you had?"

PUPPETS—Present-Day

Purpose: That children use puppets to:
- express feelings and actions of present-day people as they (the children) think through problem situations;
- demonstrate ways of obeying God's commands and acting on God's promises.

Materials
☐ Present-day puppets (children can make their own or use puppets from Puppet Box)—see pages 54-56.
☐ Stage (optional)—see page 56.

Procedure
1. Read a Bible verse.
2. Guide children to (a) tell about situations when they need to remember this Bible verse; (b) select one situation to act out. Or, suggest an open-ended situation (a problem situation that needs to be solved in light of this verse).
3. Guide children to think through the situation by asking questions:
   a. What happens first?
   b. Who are the people? What do they say?
   c. How do they feel? How can you show this?
   d. What happens next?
4. List the people needed as children identify them. Decide who will play each character.
5. Children either make simple puppets or choose puppets from Puppet Box.
6. Children use puppets to act out the story. If a child pauses, ask a question to help him/her remember the action of the story.
7. Guide children to evaluate the results by asking questions such as, "How did (name of puppet) obey/not obey the Bible command we read? What's another way he/she might have obeyed this command? What are some ways you can obey this command at home? at school? at church?"

Variations
1. Children can use present-day puppets to interview a missionary or children from other countries.
2. Children can make and use puppets for a choir. Example: Make puppets of children of different races and use them for a puppet choir to sing "God Loves Each Child" (number 42 in *Sing to the Lord,* Praise Books, GL Publications).

Guided Conversation
Example of an open-ended situation for use in teaching Leviticus 19:11—"Your mother sent you to the store for some groceries. On the way home, you discover the clerk gave you too much money back. What will you do?"

PUPPETS—How to Make Them

Puppet Box

Enlist the help of parents and other adults in making puppets and props for children to use in puppet Bible learning activities. Step-by-step instructions and patterns for puppets and props can be found in *Easy-to-Make Puppets and How to Use Them: Children/Youth,* by Fran Rottman, Regal Books, GL Publications, Ventura, CA.

Store puppets and props in a box that has been covered with colorful paper and labeled "Puppet Box."

Student-Made Puppets

Children enjoy making their own puppets. Here are several puppets they can make quickly—and that can be made into either Bible characters or present-day people. Page 56 also shows some simple staging ideas.

Tube Puppet

Materials
☐ 4½-inch (11.25 cm) length of cardboard tube (on which paper towels, foil, toilet tissue are packaged)
☐ 3x5-inch (7.5x12.5 cm) cardboard
☐ yarn for hair
☐ scissors
☐ glue
☐ construction paper/felt/fabric scraps
☐ crayons or felt pens
☐ 5-inch (12.5 cm) chenille wire

Procedure
1. Use crayons or felt pens to draw face.
2. Cut clothing pieces from felt, fabric or construction paper. Glue to tube.
3. Make hair by winding yarn around 5-inch (12.5 cm) cardboard. Remove cardboard. Tie yarn in the middle. Cut yarn loops. Spread yarn out and glue to top of tube. Trim for hair style.
4. Punch arm holes in sides of tube. Insert chenille wire. Bend wire to make hands.
5. Cut feet from construction paper and glue to tube.

Pencil Puppet

Materials
- [ ] Styrofoam ball 2 inches (5 cm) in diameter
- [ ] Pencil or 8-inch (20 cm) piece of ¼-inch (6.25 mm) dowel
- [ ] Fine-point felt pen or crayon
- [ ] Yarn
- [ ] 5-inch (12.5 cm) chenille wire
- [ ] Fabric scraps
- [ ] Glue

Procedure
1. Spread glue on point of pencil or one end of dowel. Insert into Styrofoam ball.
2. Glue yarn to ball for hair.
3. Use chenille wire for arms.
4. Add fabric for clothing.

Paper Bag Puppets

Materials
- [ ] Paper bag
- [ ] Shredded paper
- [ ] Dowel, ruler or toilet tissue roll
- [ ] Fabric
- [ ] Felt pens
- [ ] Yarn
- [ ] Glue
- [ ] String

(continued on next page)

Procedure

1. Stuff the paper bag with shredded paper.
2. Tie off the bottom and insert a dowel, ruler or tissue roll to serve as handle or finger hold.
3. Drape a piece of fabric over the stick.
4. Make hair of yarn. Draw or glue on the facial features.

Variation

1. Draw facial features on the bottom of closed paper bag, placing puppet's mouth as in second sketch.
2. Insert hand in bag. Move bag to make mouth open and close.

Puppet Stages

It is not necessary to have a puppet stage. However, simple stages are easy to provide. Puppeteers can stand behind a piano or bookcase. Or they can kneel behind a table turned on its side.

For more elaborate stages, see *Easy-to-Make Puppets and How to Use Them: Children/Youth,* by Fran Rottman, Regal Books, GL Publications, Ventura, CA.

DRAMA ACTIVITIES

ROLEPLAY

Purpose: That children:
- identify with, and understand, the feelings of others through dramatizing a problem and its resolution;
- evaluate several solutions to the problem;
- discover, through reading and applying God's Word, the best solution(s) to the problem.

Materials
☐ Cards/sheets on which are written roleplay situations related to children's current unit of Bible lessons and the personal needs of the learners. (No costumes, props or scenery are needed.)

Roleplay situations help learners clarify their response to "If I were that person, I would. . . ."

Examples of roleplay situations for older children

1. Story-starters

"You are at the store with your friends, Gerry and Marty. You see a really neat game. You each want to get a game to take home, but you have just enough money—if you put all your money together—to buy one game. Suddenly, Gerry says, 'I've got a great idea! I know how we can each get a game just by using the money we have.' As you listen to Gerry's plan, you discover it isn't honest. But Marty thinks it's a great idea. Act out this story and show how you think it should end."

"Your father tells you it's time to go to bed, but you want to stay up and watch TV. Think of all the reasons your father would give for your going to bed and all the reasons you would give for staying up. We need two people to act out what happens."

2. Questions to act out responses to

"What do you say when your best friend asks to copy your homework?"

"What can be done when your group begins 'cutting down' an unpopular girl?"

"What can you do when the gang requires that you steal some money from your parents in order to be a member of the group?"

Examples of roleplay situations for younger children

"Terry sees that Mother is very busy fixing dinner. We need someone to be Terry and someone to be Mother. Show us some 'surprise kindnesses' that Terry can do for Mother."

"You are playing a game with your friend. Your little brother kicks the game board and knocks the pieces out of place. Show us what you and your friend will do."

(continued on next page)

Procedure

1. Read or tell the situation.

2. Assign students to each part or let them volunteer. Be careful not to place a child in a role similar to his/her own personality. For instance, don't choose a shy child to play the part of a timid person.
   Note: Some children feel uneasy and self-conscious in roleplay. Encourage children, but do not force a child to participate if he is uncomfortable doing it. However, do encourage him/her to respond to the situation after roleplay.

3. Children act out the situation any way they like, whether it's a "biblically correct" solution or not.

4. Cut the action while the characters are still involved in their parts (before the children run out of something to say).

5. Interview each character. This evaluation is a key to learning. Ask each character how he felt in his role, how he wanted to react, what his feelings were toward others in the roleplay. For example, "Gerry, how did you feel when Karen said she didn't want to go along with your plan to get the game dishonestly? Karen, how did you feel when Gerry called you a coward?"

6. Involve all of the children in answering questions such as, "Was this the best solution? Why/why not? What does the Bible tell us that would help us know a good solution to this problem?" Guide the children's thinking just enough so THEY (not you!) discover solutions built upon biblical principles.

7. If it's appropriate, let the same children—or new ones—re-enact the scene, roleplaying a different solution to the problem. Again, cut the action at the appropriate place and let the children evaluate this new solution.

CHORAL SPEAKING

Purpose: That children work together to interpret a passage of Scripture, poetry or prose.

Note: The goal of choral speaking is not perfection in children's delivery. Rather, it is an appreciation for the sounds and meanings of words as they are put together.

Materials

☐ Duplicated copies of the passage (one per child) and/or a large chart with the passage lettered on it.

☐ Pens/pencils for marking the way the passage will be read.

Procedure

1. Read the passage with expression as children follow the words.
2. Let children tell in their own words what different sections of the passage mean. Explain any unfamiliar words.
3. Ask children to think about ways to make the meaning of this passage clear by the way they say it. Let children decide which sections would sound best loud/soft, fast/slow, high/low—also which words to emphasize. Mark sections to show the children's decisions. Underline words to be emphasized.
4. Guide children to decide which sections should be said by individuals (solos), small groups, the entire group. Mark sections.
5. Assign parts to individuals and small groups.
6. Children say the passage the way they decided on.
7. Talk about whether or not the choral reading made the meaning of the passage clear. (Children may want to try some sections several ways.) Decide on changes that need to be made.
8. Children say the passage again, with the changes they decided on.
9. Consider presenting this passage for another group (in your school, church or an outside organization such as a convalescent home).

Example: Psalm 100 (*NIV*)

ALL: Shout for joy to the LORD, all the earth. (fast, enthusiastic)
Solo 1: Serve the Lord with gladness;
Solo 2: Come before him with joyful songs.
ALL: Know that the LORD is God. (slow, deliberate, emphatic)
Solo 3: It is he who made us, and we are his;
Solo 4: We are his people, the sheep of his pasture.
Group A: Enter his gates with thanksgiving (louder, lower voices)
Group B: And his courts with praise (softer—echo effect)
Group A: Give thanks to him (louder, lower voices)
Group B: And praise his name (softer—echo effect)
Solo 5: For the Lord is good (slowly, softly, deliberately)
Group A: And his love endures forever; (louder)
ALL: His faithfulness continues (louder)
    Through all generations. (very loud, triumphant)

ORAL COMMUNICATION

Oral communication involves an ability (talking) which all children possess and with which most children feel comfortable.

Benefits

Oral communication activities allow children to
- share their needs, interests, concerns, understanding (and misunderstandings), and possible solutions to problems.
- be heard by someone who will listen actively and attentively to what he/she is saying. (Children are often with people who only hear their words, but do not listen with understanding to what a child is saying.)
- increase their listening skills.
- improve their Bible memory skills.

Tips

1. When a child or group of children tend to dominate an oral activity, set guidelines. For example, "Tom, we like to hear your good ideas, but we need to hear from two other people before you talk again."
2. Give gentle encouragement to a child who is hesitant to participate.
   - Begin by asking him/her a non-threatening question requiring a minimum answer (for example, a question like "What flavor ice cream do you like best, vanilla or chocolate?") Then share his/her response: "Pat thinks chocolate ice cream tastes best."
   - Suggest that each child turn to the person next to him/her to talk over a question or an idea. For example, "Tell your neighbor one way you obeyed your mother this past week."

60

ORAL COMMUNICATION

CONVERSATION

Purpose: That children increase information and understanding as they interact verbally with each other and with adults in the classroom.

Materials
☐ Bibles
☐ Books and/or pictures related to the conversation topic (optional)
☐ Tape recorder and blank cassette (optional)
☐ Chalkboard and chalk or chart paper and felt pens (optional)

Procedure
1. Provide an atmosphere of acceptance in which children feel comfortable to share their ideas and to question. You can do this by:
   - Showing interest in students' interests and concerns;
   - Sharing from your own experiences—both successes and failures;
   - Inviting questions and suggestions;
   - Affirming children when they contribute ideas and suggestions.
2. Begin the conversation in one of several ways.
   - Ask a question that will stimulate thought and conversation.
   - Respond to, and encourage, a conversation started by a child.
   - Record a question on a blank cassette and encourage children to record their responses.
   - Letter a question or some key words on the chalkboard or on a piece of chart paper. Suggest that children talk about the question and/or words.
3. Work on developing the skill of active listening. Conversation must have talkers and listeners. The roles change so that within a very short period of time everyone will be able to talk and to listen. Active listeners do these things.
   - Listen to the person who is speaking.
   - Look at the person who is speaking.
   - Wait for a turn to talk (do not interrupt).
   - Restate or rephrase the speaker's main point before introducing your ideas.

The result will be that everyone will want to be a part of the conversation and will feel accepted as a result of his/her ideas being accepted.

Variations
1. Record the conversation on a cassette so that it can be used as a resource for other Bible learning activities.
2. Take notes of important ideas to be used later in other Bible learning activities.

Guided Conversation Ideas
Ask "How," "What," "When," and "Why" questions to stimulate thinking. Avoid questions that can be answered with "Yes" or "No." There is no quicker way to end a conversation or discussion. Resist the temptation to label a statement as "wrong." If inaccurate information is shared, find the correct information in a way that is accepting of the child who shared the misinformation. This is an excellent way to use informal conversation to correct misunderstandings.

DISCUSSION

Purpose: That children participate in a give-and-take oral activity as they discover answers to questions, determine solutions for problems and share ideas.

Materials
☐ Bibles (to be used to check information as needed)
☐ Blank paper or chalkboard to record conclusions for reference

Procedure
1. Arrange seating in a circle or semi-circle so that participants may look at each other. Use chairs or a floor area.
2. The adult(s) need to be part of the group in the circle.
3. Use stimulating comments/questions to start the discussion. For example, to start a discussion about how to show love by being a good friend, you might ask the question, "What are some things you look for in a friend—what can you expect of a friend?"
4. All oral contributions need to be accepted with respect.
5. Encourage participation as children feel comfortable and want to contribute rather than directing a question to a specific child.
6. Encourage those who dominate a discussion to allow others to participate by saying something like, "We like your good ideas, Tom. Now perhaps you would like to know what Jim thinks about it."
7. Summarize the discussion. Pull together the ideas discussed. Everyone may not agree with the summary, but at least it will be possible to know the highlights of the discussion.
8. Record key ideas on a chart for future reference.

Variations
1. *Speaker-Discussion* combines research, interview, and discussion and is greatly enjoyed by older children. A speaker is invited to make a presentation. Prior to the visit, the children prepare questions to ask. Following the presentation, children and speaker participate in a discussion period.
2. Older children may enjoy participating in a *panel discussion*. Select four children to serve as panel members. An adult needs to act as moderator to keep the discussion going. Let the children know ahead of time the topic they will be discussing so that they will be ready to share ideas and information or opinions. When the panel members are through with their presentation, other children may add to the discussion.

Guided Conversation Ideas
Encourage acceptance of ideas by statements such as: "I like your good ideas. Can someone think of other answers to the question?" "It really is hard to make friends in a new school. Tell us something you have tried that has helped." "How do you feel when that happens to you? What can you do about it?"

ORAL COMMUNICATION

BRAINSTORMING

Purpose: That children share many ideas as rapidly as possible.

Materials
☐ Chalkboard and chalk, or
☐ Newsprint or shelf paper and felt pens

Procedure
1. The teacher presents a problem or a question to the group. For example: "Let's think of as many ways as possible that we can show the love of Jesus to people around us."
2. Set a time limit of 3 to 5 minutes.
3. Children respond in turn as quickly as possible. The responses move back and forth from one to another. Children may respond more than once. Every contribution is accepted and no evaluation is made.
4. As ideas are given, they need to be recorded on the chalkboard or paper. An adult may record for younger children. Fourth, fifth, and sixth graders will enjoy doing their own recording. You may have a "recording team" with two children recording, each taking alternate responses.
5. Read the responses. Evaluate and use the ideas that are most appropriate for the situation.

Variations
1. Use brainstorming to plan a Bible learning activity. "What are some things we want to include in our mural?"
2. Reinforce some Bible information. "What are some things Jesus did to help people who came to Him?"
3. Plan for a way to use Bible truth in daily situations. "What will you do this week to be a good friend?" Following the brainstorming and evaluation, select one idea and plan to put it into practice during the week with some accountability to report results at the next class period.

Guided Conversation Ideas
The opportunity for demonstrating acceptance of the ideas of others is one of the strengths of the brainstorming process. Plan for several ways to do this. During the evaluation at the end, use statements like, "These are good ideas. Which one will you choose to try?" "There are so many ways to respond to every situation. You have a long list of good ideas."

BUZZ GROUPS

Purpose: That children have an opportunity to discuss a question or topic in a small group and then stretch their learning as the groups share with the total group.

Materials
☐ Bibles (to check ideas and information)
☐ Paper and pencils (to record ideas and plan report)

Procedure
1. Divide group into small groups of three to five children. They may number off 1-2-3, 1-2-3 and then the ones form a group, twos form a group, etc. Or they may just pull chairs around into small groups.
2. Assign each group a question or topic. They may each have the same question/topic or different ones that are related to each other.
3. Allow about five minutes for buzzing. Then ask each group to report to the total group.

Variations
1. Ask the youngest child in each group to be ready to report—or the one who has a birthday nearest to Christmas. It is important that someone in the group accept the responsibility for reporting.
2. If the topic is one that is being considered in another Bible learning activity, the reports may be recorded on cassette for future reference.

Guided Conversation Ideas
"Are you lying if you do not tell the truth because it might offend someone?" "Is waiting for awhile to obey your parents the same thing as disobeying?" "What things tell you of God's love for you every day?"

CIRCLE RESPONSE

Purpose: That children be involved in a discussion experience in which every person in the group will participate.

Materials
☐ Circle of chairs, or
☐ Floor area in which the children can sit in a circle
☐ Chalkboard and chalk (optional)

Procedure
1. Ask children to sit in a circle.
2. Ask a question for children to respond to (see "Guided Conversation Ideas").
3. Explain that children will respond in turn, going around the circle.
4. They are not to respond to another person's statement until the second time around the circle. Then they may ask a question of another participant.
5. Use circle response during a variety of discussion times. Keep it in mind as a simple procedure which allows every learner the opportunity to respond to, and consider, the responses of others—since a person cannot speak until it is his/her turn around the circle again.

Variations
1. Use circle response when the question or topic may be controversial. Everyone will be able to respond comfortably.
2. Circle response is a helpful tool when the conversation or discussion is dominated by one or a few learners, or when one or more rarely contribute.

Guided Conversation Ideas
Plan or structure questions so that they require some thought and evaluation on the part of the learners. Analytical questions encourage learners to combine meanings with facts; personal questions guide the learners in decision making. "What are some reasons why David was not afraid to face Goliath?" "If you had been David, what would you have done when the king gave you his armor?"

65

QUESTION AND ANSWER

Purpose: That learners respond to questions about a Scripture passage or about the application of Bible truth in their lives.

Materials
☐ Bibles
☐ Paper and pencils (optional)

Procedure
1. The teacher prepares questions based upon the section of Scripture being studied. (Questions with definite right and wrong answers are sometimes helpful to discover what learners know about a subject, but they also tend to limit participation by many children. Interest and involvement by all students increases when teachers pose questions that ask for opinions, evaluations, feelings, or other areas in which more than one answer is acceptable.)
2. Questions may be asked during the Bible study time or any other appropriate segment of class.
3. Learners may work individually, in small groups, or as a total group to answer the questions.

Variations
1. Answers may be written and shared later during the session.
2. Use questions to assist learners as they plan their Bible learning activity.
3. Learners may work in small groups to read a Scripture passage and to write questions to ask other learners or small groups.

Guided Conversation Ideas
Informational questions require the learner to remember specific facts: "Where did Moses live as a child?" *Analytical questions* encourage learners to attach meaning to the facts: "What do you think Moses said when _____?" *Personal questions* help the learners explore their own attitudes and values: "How would you decide the right thing to do in this situation?"

ORAL COMMUNICATION

CASE STUDY

Purpose: That learners respond to a real-life experience.

Materials
☐ Prepared case studies (see "Sample Situations" below)
☐ Bibles (to check references that apply to the situations)

Procedure
1. Prepare case studies before class time. These may be suggested by learners and teachers.
2. Read the case study. It needs to involve a situation that is within the realm of the learners' experience.
3. Lead children to discuss what happened. Explore some alternative actions.

Variations
1. Record the case study on cassette so that a portion of the group can work with it during an activity time.
2. Respond to the situation by acting out alternative solutions.

Sample Situations
1. Helen's mother asked her to take care of her little brother. She asked Helen to stay in the backyard to play with him.
   Two of Helen's friends came by and asked her to come out in front to play softball with them. Helen would really like to play softball. What should she do?
   ● Take her brother out in front to watch the friends play softball.
   ● Invite her friends to play in the backyard.
   ● Go in the house and ask Mother if she could go out front.
   What are some other things Helen might decide to do?

2. Al and Tim want to become part of the school baseball team. They really need to practice those pitches! One day they were throwing the ball back and forth when it slipped and went through a window in Mr. Horton's garage door! Both boys were surprised!
   "It's your fault," said Al.
   "You should have caught the ball!" said Tim.
   Al replied with, "How could I with that crummy throw!"
   Tim and Al notice that Mr. Horton is coming around through the yard to see what happened. What should they do?
   ● Run as fast as they can and hope that Mr. Horton does not see them.
   ● Say that Tim threw the ball.
   ● Say that Al did it.
   What are some other things Al and Tim might decide to do?

Guided Conversation Ideas
"What might happen if _____?" "Name some other things that you might do." "What action would be the best for the whole group?"

WORD ASSOCIATION

Purpose: That children respond with the first word or idea that comes to mind when a word or phrase is presented to them, as a way of introducing/exploring a topic.

Materials
☐ Chalkboard and chalk or newsprint and felt pens (optional)

Procedure
1. Say a word or phrase that is related to the study for the session.
2. Ask children to tell what they think of first when they hear the word or phrase.
3. Use their responses to draw conclusions, to compare ideas or to lead into the study for the day. Word association will assist you in finding out what the learners already know about a topic or what they feel about it.

Guided Conversation Ideas
"Say a word that describes how you feel when you hear this word. Say the first thing you think of. If you have another idea, say it after several others in the group have responded."

STORYTELLING

Purpose: That the learners will have an opportunity to participate in telling the Bible story.

Materials
☐ Bibles
☐ Paper and pencils (optional—older children may wish to use them)
☐ Pictures (optional)

Procedure
1. Assist children in the selection of the Bible story that they will prepare to tell.
2. The story may be told to another small group within the class or to a group of younger children.
3. Children may wish to combine this activity with an art activity by making simple illustrations or puppets to help to tell the story.
4. Provide time to practice the story.
5. Arrange for the storytelling time and place.

Variations
1. Provide a tape recorder and blank cassette. Learners may record their Bible stories. The stories can be shared with absent children or kept in the room for a resource for a Bible learning activity.
2. The tape and tape recorder can be used in a listening center.
3. Learners may read stories from a book. The reading can be taped, including a sound such as a soft bell or click to tell the listeners when to turn the page.

Guided Conversation Ideas
Encourage learners to be aware of sequence by asking, "What happened next?" Help the storytellers include some dialogue in their stories by asking, "What did _____ say when _____?" "What does this story help us understand about something God wants us to do?" will encourage the learners to think about the application of Bible truth in their daily lives.

INTERVIEW A BIBLE PERSON

Purpose: That the learners will review, discover, and summarize information about a Bible person.

Materials
- ☐ Bibles
- ☐ Paper and pencil

Procedure
1. Let one of the learners (or a teacher or guest) take the part of the Bible person that is involved in your study.
2. A small group (3-4) learners can prepare questions to ask the "Bible person."
3. The rest of the class can be observers of this process.
4. At the completion of the interview, the observers may question the "Bible person."

Variations
1. The Bible person may wear a simple costume.
2. The interview may be recorded and used as a research tool.

Guided Conversation Ideas
Encourage children to ask questions about feelings as well as about events. If the Bible person was Paul, some questions might be, "What did you do while you were watching the stoning of Stephen?" "How did you feel when you were blind?" "What was a hard thing about becoming a follower of Jesus?" "What was a blessing that came to you as a result of following Jesus?"

ORAL COMMUNICATION

OPEN-ENDED SITUATION

Purpose: That children have an opportunity to think through ways of applying Bible truths to daily living.

Materials
☐ Bibles (may be used to check ideas and informations)
☐ Paper and pencils (optional)
☐ Drawing paper and crayons or felt pens (optional)

Procedure
1. Supply open-ended (or unfinished) sentences or questions. They need to be related to situations faced by children in the group.
2. Children complete the Bible content and/or answer the statement. After everyone in the small groups participates, main ideas may be shared with the large group.
3. Responses may be shared orally, written, drawn, or dramatized.

Variations
1. Provide a box with a slit in the top and encourage children to deposit suggestions for open-ended sentences or situations. From time to time, draw out one of the suggestions and let the group respond.
2. Use open-ended statements during the planning and research time of the Bible learning activity.
3. Use open-beginning statements in which students are given a conclusion and must suggest probable beginnings.
4. Use open-middle statements in which students must suggest possible links between a beginning and a conclusion.

Guided Conversation Ideas
"A new boy/girl is in your class for the first time. Your best friend does not want to include him/her during recess time. You decide to _____." "Showing love to others is _____." "A good friend is _____." "Jesus is pleased when we _____."

CREATIVE WRITING

Creative writing activities can provide valuable learning experiences for children when the experiences are planned according to the abilities of the child and when they hold no threat of failure.

Benefits

Lesson-related creative writing activities can help children:
- list/describe specific, concrete examples of an abstract concept such as loving, forgiving, worshiping, serving;
- express their feelings about God, or about their experiences and needs;
- share Bible information they have discovered;
- crystallize their thinking as they put their ideas into words;
- record ways they put Bible truths into practice in daily life;
- show love to others (for example, writing letters to missionaries or people who are homebound, writing thank-you notes to parents or the church staff, making "I will help you" coupons in which they offer to run errands, etc.);
- improve their recall of Bible events by organizing and writing information about the Bible story.

Tips

1. Most children will want to do their own writing, but some will need help. Consider these ideas:
   - Write on chalkboard or word cards any words that children need to know how to spell;
   - Let a child record his/her thoughts on tape. Later, write or type these ideas and add them to the project being worked on;
   - Have a child dictate his/her ideas to you or an aide or another child who acts as a recorder. As a child's skills increase during the year, encourage him/her to write a portion of what he/she wants to say.
   - Let children work together, making sure one person in the group is skilled enough to record/write up the ideas of the group;
   - Let a group dictate a story or letter for you to write down.
2. A child's creative writing efforts are usually more productive when the teacher has done some "pump priming" to stimulate thinking.
   - Show/discuss pictures or objects that stimulate thinking.
   - Provide "story-starters" (partially-described situations which children build on or complete.
   - Suggest a problem for children to resolve.
   - Before children begin writing, encourage them to talk about possible ideas they might use.

CREATIVE WRITING

SENTENCES (about pictures)

Purpose: That the child tells about a picture he/she has made or is viewing.

Materials
- ☐ Pictures (made by children or from visual aids)
- ☐ Sentence strips or other strips of paper
- ☐ Felt pens

Procedure
1. Child paints, draws or sketches a picture. (Materials and procedure may be found in ART section.)
2. Pictures from visual aid packets or any other picture source may be used.
3. Listen to the child talk about the picture.
4. Children in grades 3-6 will be able to write their sentences. Some may prefer to have the teacher do the writing.
5. Children in grades 1,2 may be able to write sentences, but will probably need to be helped by teacher or older child.
6. The child decides on the sentence that he/she would like to have written about the picture. When the sentence is written, it may be stapled or taped to the picture.
7. Pictures may be mounted on a bulletin board or put up on the wall. They may be bound into a book for future reference or children may wish to take home the ones they have made.

Guided Conversation Ideas
Encourage children to discover the main idea illustrated in a picture. You may ask, "What did Abraham understand about God when he was ready to sacrifice Isaac?" If the picture is child-made, questions help to clarify thinking. "What is the most important thing about your picture? What do you want people to know about your picture?"

DICTATE (adult record)

Purpose: That the child express information, ideas and/or feelings without being inhibited by the mechanics of writing.

Materials
- ☐ Paper
- ☐ Pencils
- ☐ Typewriter (optional)
- ☐ Cassette recorder and blank tape (optional)

Procedure
1. Child talks about a picture, an item or a Bible event.
2. An adult worker records what the child says.
3. The writing may take the form of a short story, a poem, a newspaper article or a radio or TV announcement. The possibilities are almost endless.

Variations
1. The child may dictate his ideas to a tape recorder. The adult writes the child's dictation from the tape. This is an effective way to utilize the tape recorder as another adult, especially when the writing does not need to be completed on the spot.
2. The adult may type what the child is saying as it is being said. Many adults can type as fast as children talk, even though they may not be accomplished typists. The child will enjoy watching his words become print. Perhaps the child can type his/her own name.

Guided Conversation Ideas
If the child is writing about a picture or event, suggest that he/she answer the question, "What is the most important thing to know about it?" "How would you describe it?" Avoid questions that can be answered Yes or No. They do not stimulate thinking. The child may wish to read out loud in order to hear his thoughts and words.

CREATIVE WRITING

NEWSPAPER

Purpose: That the child relates his/her knowledge about a specific Bible event.

Materials
- ☐ Bibles
- ☐ Paper
- ☐ Pencils or pens
- ☐ Typewriter (optional)
- ☐ Chart paper or small index cards on which you have written Bible events and their Bible references (one Bible event per card—or a listing of events on chart).

Procedure
1. Read about the event in the Bible; talk together about the things that happened.
2. Talk about or list questions that a newspaper article could answer about the event.
3. Write the article.
4. Articles may be displayed on bulletin board or duplicated in newspaper form for distribution.

Variations
1. Select a name for the newspaper.
2. "Paste up" the copy.
3. Duplicate for class members, parents or others.
4. Newspapers may be kept in classroom for future reference.
5. Some children may wish to type their article. Adult workers could be available for typing, too.
6. Children can work in teams to report and illustrate the events.

Headlines
King Rides a Donkey!
Asleep in a Garden
Man Betrays Friend
Is Innocent Man Convicted?
Cock Crows Three Times
Alive Again!

Guided Conversation Ideas
"Imagine that you were with Jesus and His friends during Holy Week. What would your readers want to know about His entrance into Jerusalem? What happened during the celebration of the Feast? Tell about the trial proceedings."

CREATIVE WRITING

SHORT STORY

Purpose: That the child relate in the form of a short story:
- a Bible event;
- a daily activity.

Materials
☐ Bibles
☐ Paper
☐ Pencils and pens
☐ Typewriter (optional)

Procedure
1. Read Bible verses describing a Bible event.
2. Talk about the event to clarify ideas.
3. Write or type the story.
4. Stories may be bound into a book to be kept in the classroom for future reference.

Variations
1. Write stories about daily activities.
2. Duplicate stories for distribution to class members.
3. Combine the writing of short stories with an art activity so that the stories may be illustrated.

Guided Conversation Ideas
Example: If children were writing a story describing a daily activity at school, you might encourage some Bible application by asking, "What verse in the Bible can you think of that would help the person in your story?" Or, "How would John 15:12 help to solve the problem?"

CREATIVE WRITING

PRAYER

Purpose: That the child:
- express a prayer to God in writing in preparation for oral prayer;
- write a prayer to be shared with someone not present in the class.

Materials
☐ Bibles
☐ Paper
☐ Pencils or pens

Procedure
1. Read Matthew 6:9-13 and/or Psalm 106:1 to help the children to begin to think about praying.
2. Make a list of things to pray about. The list may include items for thanksgiving, names of people with special need, or needs of the child writing the prayer.
3. Encourage children to express their thoughts to God in a conversational way— much as they would talk with a good friend at school.
4. Prayers may be placed in an envelope to be opened and read during later class meetings in order to share the results of praying.
5. Help children to recognize "No," "Wait" and "Here's something better" responses to prayers as well as "Yes" answers.

Variations
1. Read prayers together in small groups after they are written.
2. As children seem to develop a comfortable feeling about praying orally, encourage them to pray from lists, or without writing.
3. From time to time, list prayer needs. Encourage children to select one or two items from the list and pray about the items they choose.

Dear God,
   I love you.
I will sHow you
my love by
being kind to
my brother.

Guided Conversation Ideas
Help children to identify prayer needs by asking questions such as, "What are some things you are thankful to have? Tell two things God provides that you need each day. Let's thank Him for some of these things." "Name someone you know who needs God's help. Ask God to help him." "How can God help you now? Talk to God about that just now."

CREATIVE WRITING

POETRY (non-poem)

Purpose: That the child express thoughts, feelings, ideas and knowledge in a simple form of poem.

Materials
- [ ] Bibles
- [ ] Paper
- [ ] Pencils or pens
- [ ] Pictures (optional)
- [ ] Typewriter (optional)

Procedure
1. Discuss topics or objects about which children wish to write some poetry.
2. Describe for the method of writing, a simple five-line, non-poem (see example below).
3. Work together to write a group poem.
4. Select nouns to be used in line 1; write individual poems.
5. The poems may be mounted and displayed on a bulletin board or they may be put in a book to be used in the room. Pages may be added to the book as more poems are written.

Variations
1. Poems may be duplicated for distribution to the group.
2. Some of the poems may be appropriately used as part of your worship time.
3. At the beginning of the year, children can become better acquainted by writing a poem about themselves to share with the group.

>   Line 1 - write a noun
>   Line 2 - two adjectives (comma between)
>   Line 3 - three verbs (comma between)
>   Line 4 - a thought or short phrase
>   Line 5 - repeat the first line
>
>   Creation
>   Mighty, planned
>   Moves, changes, grows
>   God planned for me
>   Creation

Guided Conversation Ideas
If the class is studying God's creation, ask the children to list things God made. Next ask, "What are some words that describe God's creation? What are some action words that tell about that part of creation? Write a short phrase about it. Repeat the first line. Read in Genesis, chapter 1, to find out about the time God created _____ ."

CREATIVE WRITING

PLAYS (simple script)

Purpose: That the child express, in the form of a simple play, the ideas, feelings, and conversation of people (Bible times or present day).

Materials
- ☐ Bible
- ☐ Paper
- ☐ Pencils or pens
- ☐ Chart paper/felt pen or chalkboard/chalk

Procedure
1. If the play is to be a Bible story, ask the children to read the Bible verses that tell the story. Then have them describe the action that takes place. Record on chart paper or chalkboard.
2. If the play is based on a daily life situation, ask the children to describe the action that will take place. Record on chart paper or chalkboard.
3. Ask children to write what the people would say as the action takes place.
4. Make copies of the script for the cast.

Variations
1. An adult may type the conversation as the children talk through the action.
2. Record conversations on tape for later writing or typing by an adult.

> Samaritan: Take care of this man. When I come back, I will pay you for any extra expenses.
>
> Innkeeper: I will take good care of him.

Guided Conversation Ideas
Example: If children were acting out the story of the Good Samaritan, you might ask, "What do you think the Samaritan said to the innkeeper?" Check Luke 10:35. "What might the man by the side of the road say to the Samaritan to express his feelings? How do you feel when you need help and no one is there? What are some things you can do to be helpful?"

SCRIPTS (drama, TV)

Purpose: That the child express in writing the conversation of the people in a Bible drama or TV play.

Materials
☐ Bible
☐ Paper
☐ Pencils or pens
☐ Typewriter (optional)
☐ Cassette recorder and blank cassette (optional)

Procedure
1. If the drama or TV play is to be based on a Bible story, ask the children to read the Bible verses that tell the story.
2. List the events that need to be shown in the play in order to tell the story.
3. Talk through the conversation for each event in the play.
4. Ask children to write what the people would say as the action takes place. Some children can act and talk through the play as others record the conversation.
5. Copies of the script may be duplicated for the cast.

Variations
1. An adult may type the conversation as the children talk through the action.
2. Record conversations on tape for later writing or typing by an adult.
3. Some dramas or TV plays may be based on daily activities or situations faced by the children. Play writers should emphasize the application of Bible truths to these situations.

Guided Conversation Ideas
Encourage children to feel with the Bible people as they think about the conversation for the dramas. "What would Joseph say to the men in the caravan as he was taken to Egypt?" Or explore the children's feelings in a daily life situation by using such questions as, "What would you say to a friend who was unhappy about moving to a new city?" A statement of feelings will lead to the conversation that needs to accompany the action of the drama.

DIARY

Purpose: That the child share information and/or feelings about a Bible event as he records happenings in his diary.

Materials
- ☐ Bibles
- ☐ Paper
- ☐ Pencils or pens
- ☐ Construction paper
- ☐ Stapler and staples

Procedure
1. The child needs to have information about the events being described in his diary. Information may be gained by reading the Bible, looking at pictures of the event or listening as the story is told.
2. Clarify ideas by encouraging the child to talk and to answer questions about the events.
3. When the child is ready to write, say, "Imagine that you are one of the people in the Bible story. Write in your diary to tell what happened today. Tell how you feel as well as what happened."
4. Diaries may be made by stapling sheets of paper together with a construction paper cover.

Variations
1. Children who do not enjoy writing, may wish to draw pictures of events and make a pictorial diary.
2. Diaries may be kept in class and added to throughout the unit of study.
3. Children may make diaries to take home and write in during the week. If the class is working on a unit emphasizing showing love to others, the child may record the times he attempts to show love during the week.

Guided Conversation Ideas
"Let's make a list of the events that happened during Holy Week. We will need to put them in the order that they occurred. Now imagine that you are Peter or John or Judas or any of the Bible people. Write something in your diary to tell what happened each day."

MUSIC ACTIVITIES

"Let the word of Christ richly dwell within you; with all wisdom teaching and admonishing one another with psalms and hymns and spiritual songs, singing with thankfulness in your hearts to God" (Col. 3:16). The apostle Paul emphasizes that our music is to (1) proceed from our knowledge of the words of the Lord Jesus; (2) be expressed to one another for mutual instruction and counsel; and (3) be addressed to God in heartfelt thankfulness. The "psalms" were those of the Old Testament, and the "hymns" were Christian compositions of praise and adoration to God. The "spiritual songs" were expressions of personal Christian experience, a form of folk music.*

Benefits

A Bible learning activity involving music is an enjoyable way for children to be actively involved in learning and remembering scriptural truths. Music carefully selected for a specific purpose can help a child:
- learn Bible truths or doctrine;
- memorize Scripture verses;
- suggest and reinforce Christian conduct;
- create an atmosphere of quietness and worship;
- move smoothly from one activity to another;
- enjoy relaxation and activity.

Music Resources

Smith, Barbara and Charles. *The Non-Musician's Guide to Children's Music* (an ICL Concept book), Ventura, CA: GL Publications, 1977.

Self, Margaret, ed. *Sing to the Lord* (songbook), Ventura, CA: Praise Book, 1976.

Self, Margaret, ed. *Sing Praises* (songbook), Ventura, CA: Praise Book, 1979.

Music cassettes with selected songs from the above two songbooks: *Songs for Middlers, Songs for Juniors,* Ventura, CA: GL Publications, 1981.

* William L. Hooper, *Church Music in Transition* (Nashville: Broadman Press, 1963), pp. 21,22.

HOW TO SELECT APPROPRIATE SONGS

Ask the following six questions about any song you intend to use. (Some songs, like "just for fun" songs, may be useful even though not all these questions can be answered yes.)

☐ **1. Is the meaning obvious to children?**

Look for songs that are self-explanatory. Keep in mind that children, especially younger ones, think literally, not symbolically. Songs such as "Climb, Climb Up Sunshine Mountain" or "This Little Light of Mine" have little meaning for children. Symbolic phrases that seem simple to adults, are often confusing to children ("I was sinking deep in sin," "Come into my heart," "Let us go to the house of the Lord").

☐ **2. Is it easily singable?**

Children respond best to simple melody lines that are repeated. Also look for songs that are within the children's range: primarily within the six note span from Middle C up to A.

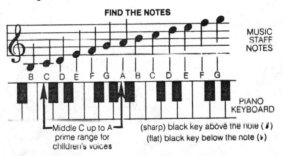

FIND THE NOTES

MUSIC STAFF NOTES

PIANO KEYBOARD

Middle C up to A—
prime range for
children's voices

(sharp) black key above the note (♯)
(flat) black key below the note (♭)

A few notes in a song may extend outside that range, but most of the melody should be within this range. Fifth and sixth grade boys who "just won't sing" are often reacting to notes that their changing voices cannot reach easily.

☐ **3. Does the song relate to the current unit of Bible lessons?**

Songs should support the aims for a unit of lessons, thus being able to be used several times in succession.

☐ **4. Are the words scripturally and doctrinally correct?**

Read the words carefully, and check them against the Scriptures.

☐ **5. Does the song build positive attitudes?**

Evaluate the mood that is created by the words, melody and rhythm. Is it consistent with your teaching goals?

☐ **6. Will children enjoy it?**

GROUP SINGING—Antiphonal

Purpose: That children express, as a group, their praise to the Lord.

Materials
☐ Songbook such as those listed on page 82
☐ Chart with song lettered on it (may be illustrated)

Procedure
1. Talk about the meaning of the words of the song.
2. Explain that you will be singing this song in the way people in Bible times often sang their songs as they worshiped at the Temple. You will divide into two groups. One group will sing a phrase and then the second group will sing a phrase.
3. Children listen to song on record, tape or sung by two teachers.
4. Sing the song antiphonally (in two groups as illustrated in the example below).

Example: Come and Praise the Lord Our King
(number 13 in *Sing to the Lord,* listed on page 82)
Group 1: Come and praise the Lord our King,
Group 2: Hallelujah!
Group 1: Lift your voice and let us sing,
Group 2: Hallelujah!

Variations of Group Singing
Here are some other enjoyable group singing activities. See *The Non-Musician's Guide to Children's Music* (listed on page 82) for instructions and examples.
1. Sing a song as a round.
2. Sing a dialogue or question and answer.
3. Chart a psalm as in Bible times.
4. Sing an astinato (ah-stin-AH-toe) with a song. An astinato is a simple melodic phrase that is played or sung over and over.
5. Sing songs in other languages.
6. Add motions to songs.
7. Choral speaking: children speak the words of the song as a verse choir (see "Choral Speaking" on page 59).

INSTRUMENTS—Bells

Purpose: That children use bells as a means of expressing praise God.

Materials
☐ Songbooks such as *Sing to the Lord* and *Sing Praises,* listed on page 82.
☐ Bells and song charts

Select and use one of the following sets of bells:

- **Melodé bells** (8 plastic bells, from F to F, each a different color). Make song charts with colored notes (gummed dots or circles cut from construction paper) above the words to indicate which color bell is to be played.

Many songs in the key of F (one flat in key signature) may be played on these bells; for example:

From *Sing to the Lord*
"Oh, How I Love Jesus" (66)
From *Sing Praises*
"God Is So Good" (30)—transpose to the key of F
"Hallelujah, Christ Is Risen" (99)
"Christ Is Risen, Sing Alleluia" (100)
"Jesus Christ Is Risen Today" (101)

- **Chromatic 20-bell set** (similar to a small xylophone; includes sharps and flats). Any simple melody with a range from middle C to G in the octave above can be played. Each bell note is clearly marked with its note letter. Make song charts with note letters above words.

- **Tone educator bells** (bars attached to separate plastic or wooden blocks and struck with mallots). They can be used in the same way as the chromatic bells. Each bell can be taken out of the box and given to a child to play.

(continued on next page)

- Octave bells and step bells (8-bell sets with a range of C to C). They can be used in some of the ways listed above, but are limited to songs in the key of C (no sharps or flats in the key signature); for example:

From *Sing Praises*
"Alleluia" (7)
"Praise Ye the Lord" (17)
"He Cares for Me" (25)

Note: Three good sources for musical instruments are:
1. Beckley-Cardy, 1900 N. Narragansett Ave., Chicago, IL 60639 / phone (312) 622-5420.
2. Children's Book and Music Center, 2500 Santa Monica Blvd., Santa Monica, CA 90404 / phone (213) 829-0215.
3. Ward Music, Ltd., 412 W. Hastings St., Vancouver, BC V6B IL3 / phone (604) 682-5288

Procedure
1. Demonstrate how to use the bells.
2.* Select children to play the bells; give one bell to each child. Have child play his/her bell whenever you point to that note (identified by color or letter) on chart.
3.* These children give their bells to other children, who then take their turn.
4. When children are familiar enough with the bells, choose a child to do as you did in pointing to the notes on the chart.
5. When children are familiar with the bells, provide this as an individual activity—one child plays the song all the way through, using the appropriate bells.
6. Consider letting children use bells to play several songs for another group (in your school, church or an outside organization such as a convalescent home).

Variations
1. Use the bells to highlight certain parts of a song, such as in these songs from *Sing to the Lord:*
"Easter Song" (165)—play bells on the phrase "bells are ringing."
"Rejoice, Rejoice! Emmanuel" (174)—play bells on the four notes for "rejoice, rejoice."
2. Children can use the bells to pick out original tunes.
3. For younger children, you can color-code bells that are not already color-coded by placing matching colors of paper or tape on the chart and the specific bells you are using.

Guided Conversation Ideas
Examples: "Psalm 150 tells us we can use instruments to praise the Lord—to tell how great God is and how much we love Him." Or, "First John 4:19 says 'We love, because He first loved us.' Let's show our love for Jesus by using these bells to play 'Oh, How I Love Jesus.' "

* Steps 2 and 3 under "Procedure" are for melode bells and tone educator bells only, since these bells can be given to individual children.

MUSIC ACTIVITIES

INSTRUMENTS—Autoharp

Purpose: That children use an autoharp as an accompaniment to songs that support their current unit of Bible study.

Materials
☐ Autoharp
☐ Songbooks that have autoharp chord markings above the staff—such as *Sing to the Lord* and *Sing Praises*, listed on page 82. Note: These chord markings are sometimes transposed to a different key than the one in which the musical score is written since autoharps have a limited number of keys and chords.
☐ Autoharp cards
  • Cut pages from an extra songbook; glue them on cardboard.
  • Or, letter the words of the song on a large index card as in sketch. Letters above words indicate chord bar to press. Slanted marks indicate when to strum the strings. Time signature and beginning note are indicated at the left.

$\frac{4}{4}$ (c) |God is so/good, |God is so/good,

|God is so/good, He's so |good to |me.

Procedure
1. To teach children how to play the autoharp, choose a short, simple (using only 2 or 3 chords), familiar song.
2. Show children how to strum the autoharp:
  • Place fingers of left hand on the chord bar buttons that will be used. In "God Is So Good," finger 1 goes on C, finger 2 goes on G7, and finger 3 goes on F.

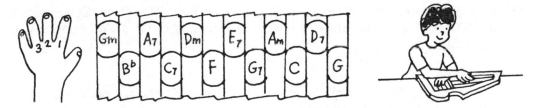

  • Press each button as indicated on song card. Cross over with your right hand and strum the strings from bottom to top.
3. Pluck string for beginning note to get your pitch for singing. For this song, you would pluck the string C. Strum autoharp as children sing.
4. Let children take turns strumming autoharp as rest of group sings.

Guided Conversation Ideas
Example: "Isaiah 63:7 (NIV) says, 'I will tell of the kindnesses of the Lord,. . .yes, the many good things he has done.' What are some kind, good things the Lord has done for you?" After children respond, say, "Let's praise God for how good He is by singing 'God Is So Good.' "

INSTRUMENTS—Zither

Purpose: That children use a zither as a means of expressing their praise to the Lord.

Materials
☐ Songbooks such as *Sing to the Lord* and *Sing Praises,* listed on page 82
☐ Zither (a stringed instrument that may have some similarity to the stringed instruments mentioned in the Bible).
☐ Zither song cards
  Cut cards to the shape of the zither. Slip a card under the strings and mark it with dots to indicate which string is to be plucked for each note of the song. Open notes are held longer than filled-in notes. Connect the dots to indicate the order in which the notes are to be played.

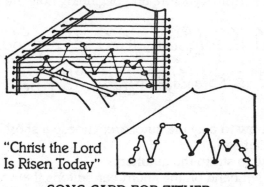

"Christ the Lord Is Risen Today"

SONG CARD FOR ZITHER

Note: A good source for zithers is the Baptist Book Store Mail Order Center, Dock 4—107 Tenth Ave., North (P.O. Box 24420) Nashville, TN 37202 / phone (615) 251-2094.

Procedure
1. Show children how to play the zither—pluck the string above each dot.
2. Let children practice using the zither.
3. Give children opportunities to play special numbers on the zither as part of your worship time or for programs in your school, church or a convalescent home.

Guided Conversation Ideas
Example: To introduce the zither, you might say, "The Bible tells us some ways we can praise God. What does Psalm 150:4 say?" Children respond. "In Bible times people had several kinds of stringed instruments. What are some stringed instruments we have today?" Children respond, naming such instruments as guitars, autoharps, violins, etc. "The zither is another kind of stringed instrument. The stringed instruments in Bible times may have been something like this. Let's use the zither to play a song of praise to God."

MUSIC ACTIVITIES

REBUS SONGS

Purpose: That children illustrate a song in a way that helps them think about and remember the words and meaning of the song.

Materials
- [ ] Songbook such as *Sing to the Lord* or *Sing Praises*, listed on page 82.
- [ ] Chart paper
- [ ] Felt pens or crayons
- [ ] Drawing paper
- [ ] Scissors
- [ ] Glue
- [ ] Song recorded on tape (optional)

Procedure
1. Select a song that has easily-pictured words.
2. Letter the words on chart paper, leaving blank spaces where children will substitute pictures for words. Here's an example from "Praise to God," no. 6 in *Sing to the Lord.*

    Praise to God for things we see,

    Growing   , waving   .

    Mother's   , the bright blue   .

3. Have children watch song chart to discover what the missing words are as (1) you read/sing all the words; or (2) they listen to a recording of the song; or (3) they read words from songbook.
4. List the missing words as children name them.
5. Decide who will draw a picture for each missing word.
6. Children draw pictures, cut them out and glue them to chart.

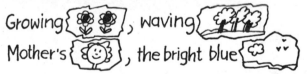

7. Children use the chart as they praise God by singing this song.

Variation
Use this as an independent activity by providing instructions on a task card or cassette tape.

Guided Conversation Ideas
Example: To introduce "Praise to God," you might say, "What are some things you're especially glad God made for you to see and enjoy?" Children respond. "This song (point to chart) tells about some things God made. Listen to find out what the missing words are."

CREATE NEW SONGS

Purpose: That children write words and/or music to express/reinforce/apply Bible truths they are learning.

Materials
☐ Songbooks such as *Sing to the Lord* and *Sing Praises,* listed on page 82.
☐ Chalkboard/chalk, or newsprint/felt pens, or overhead projector/transparencies/pens
☐ Cassette tapes with music recorded on them (optional)

Procedure
Begin with this very simple idea, then move to more challenging ones (see "Variations" below). The numbers in parentheses on this page and the next page refer to song numbers in *Sing to the Lord.*
1. Select a song with a simple, familiar tune—for example, "Tell Me the Stories of Jesus" (56).
2. Write new words based on the Bible story/verse/passage you are studying.
3. Letter the words on a song chart, leaving blank spaces for children to fill in:
    Tell me the story of (Moses), How he was (brave).
    Tell how he went to see (Pharaoh), God's people were (slaves).
    Scenes in the (desert), Crossing the (sea).
    Stories of (Moses), Tell them to me.
4. Fill in words as children suggest them.
5. Sing the song.

Variations
1. **Let children create a new phrase or sentence for a song.**
    For example, if you are using the song "How Do You You Obey God's Word" (101), follow these steps:

    ● Sing the first stanza as it is written.
        How do you obey God's Word?
        How do you obey God's Word?
        I cheerfully do what my parents say;
        That's how I obey God's Word.

    ● Ask, "What are some things your parents ask you to do?" When children have suggested several ideas, select one or two ideas to sing in place of the third line. Here are some examples:
        I take out the trash and rake the leaves.
        I make my bed and clean up my room.
        I go to bed when my parents say.

    ● Sing the song with the new words.

(continued on next page)

- Sing it again, acting out the new words as you sing (optional).
- Create and sing more new words.
  Additional songs that can be used in this way:
    "My Prayer" (116)
    "How Do You Show Love for the Lord?" (131)
    "Come, Let Me Tell" (137). This song is also on *Songs for Middlers, cassette A,* listed on page 82.

2. **Guide children in adding a stanza to a known song.**
   For example, if you are studying James 1:22 and want to write additional words to the tune of "Lord, I Want to Be a Christian" (142), you might follow these steps:

   - Ask children to suggest some things they need to ask God to help them do in order to be "doers of the Word." List these as children suggest them.

   - Have children hum the tune, or listen to it on tape, as they clap the rhythm. (Instrumental music for this song is on the cassette *Songs for Juniors, cassette A,* listed on page 82.)

   - Let children suggest words. Adapt words to fit the rhythm.
     For example,
         Lord, I want to be more ready to obey (forgive), to obey (forgive), etc.
     Lord, I want to be more cheerful (helpful, loving) in my home (church, school), etc.

   - Sing the new verse.
     Additional songs that can be used in this way:
         "Come and Praise the Lord Our King" (13)
         "Be Thankful Unto Him" (15)
         "God Is So Good" (41)
         "God's Word I Will Obey" (95)
         "Lord, I Thank You" (118)
3. **Help children set a Bible verse to music.***
4. **Help children compose a new song.***
5. **Guide children in writing a Bible ballad.***

Guided Conversation Ideas

Example: To motivate children to write their own song of praise to God, you might say, "The Bible tells us, 'Sing to the Lord a new song, for he has done marvelous things' (Psalm 98:1, *NIV*). God enjoys hearing our songs of praise—songs that have already been written and songs that we write ourselves. What are some things you want to praise God for?"

* See instructions in *The Non-Musician's Guide to Children's Music,* listed on page 82.

RESEARCH ACTIVITIES

Children need to develop research skills in order to more effectively discover and apply Bible truths.

Benefits

Research activities help children:
- develop skill in using their Bibles to locate information;
- develop skill in using Bible study resources such as maps, atlases, concordances, Bible dictionaries;
- develop skill in working together to find information;
- discover the meanings of new words and phrases;
- gather information they need about a particular topic;
- explore feelings (for example, discussing the feelings of people in a film can lead them to share/discuss their own feelings about a topic or question).

Tips

1. Provide resources that can be used by children with a wide range of abilities. For example,
   - information recorded on tape;
   - pictures and well-illustrated books;
   - resource cards and Bible dictionaries that require varying degrees of ability;
   - films, filmstrips, objects and field trips.
2. Demonstrate the use of resources.
3. Give simple "practice" assignments for developing research skills before expecting children to use these skills in Bible learning activities. For example, make sure children know how to use the distance scale on a map before expecting them to measure distances as part of a Bible learning activity.

BOOKS

Purpose: That the children have opportunities to use a wide variety of books to gain information. Information should not only add to their knowledge, but should help them to complete Bible learning activities.

Materials
- [ ] Books
- [ ] Book rack or shelves for storage
- [ ] Comfortable, inviting place to read (pillows, book nook, loft, etc.)

Procedure
1. Provide a variety of attractive books related to unit Bible learning aim.
2. Select books for children with a wide range of reading skills.
3. Change books each unit.
4. Place construction paper markers in books to assist children in locating information.
5. Use the church school and public library as sources of books.
6. Encourage children to use books to locate information they need to complete activities.
7. Beginning readers need books with illustrations from which they can gather accurate information.

Variations
1. Encourage teachers and children to bring books to share with the class.
2. Build a classroom library. Each classroom needs several Bibles; consider a variety of translations, Bible dictionaries, etc.
3. From time to time, it may be possible to add some of the children's writings to the "library."

Guided Conversation Ideas
"Elisha helped a mother have enough oil for her family and enough to sell to earn money she needed to pay a debt. See how many different ways oil was used in Bible times. Use the dictionaries, storybooks or pictures in the books to find out about oil."

BIBLE READING

Purpose: That children:
- develop a pattern of daily Bible reading;
- use their Bibles in class to locate information.

Materials
☐ Bibles
☐ Paper, pencils and construction paper to make a "Bible Reading Diary" (optional)

Procedure
1. Plan for ways to make Bible reading an integral part of every class session.
2. On the chalkboard, a chart or index cards, make a list of Bible references that will be read during the class period.
3. Have children locate the Bible passage containing the Bible story. Have them locate and read the Bible verse to be memorized.
4. Encourage some Bible reading during the week. The learners may enjoy keeping a "Bible reading diary." Ask them to record ideas and thoughts about the verses they read. (Urge learners to focus on ideas they do understand and not to get bogged down when they come to parts they do not understand.)

Variations
1. Prepare Bible reading response sheets to be used by the learners. Include questions about events, feelings and ideas. Encourage learners to add their questions to the sheet.
2. Record Bible passages on cassette for reluctant readers to use.

Guided Conversation Ideas
"Find the words that tell us two things that Jesus wants us to do." "Which verse tells us that Abraham trusted God?"

BIBLE STUDY TEAMS

Purpose: That children work as a team to study a portion of Scripture.

Materials
☐ Bibles
☐ Assigned passage of Scripture
☐ Paper and pencils

Procedure
1. Divide the class into two groups. It is helpful if both groups have some skilled readers and some less capable readers.
2. One team is assigned to read and study the passage and to list questions to be asked of the other team.
3. The second team is asked to read and study the passage in order to be able to answer the questions posed by the first team.
4. Provide some class time for the study. Work may be continued at home.
5. Reverse roles so that those asking the questions will answer them another time.

Variations
1. Record questions and answers on blank cassette to be kept for future reference.
2. Provide a variety of translations of the Bible. Encourage learners to compare the translations. Look for words that mean the same thing. Locate the shortest way to make a statement.

Guided Conversation Ideas
"Find the verse that answers my question." "Let's talk about several ways to say the same thing." "Match the action word with the person who is talking."

LOOK AND LISTEN TEAMS

Purpose: That children share the responsibility for gaining information as they look at and listen to a presentation.

Materials
☐ Equipment that is needed to show selected materials
☐ Material selected for listening and viewing (film, filmstrip, etc.)
☐ Response sheets (optional)

Procedure
1. Set up equipment and selected material.
2. Divide the class into two, three or four small groups.
3. Assign each group a specific thing to discover as they view the presentation.
4. Each group shares its information with the total class group.
5. Response sheets may be used to provide specific questions.

Variations
1. Ask children to imagine that each of them is one of the people in the film or filmstrip. Share information and feelings from the viewpoint of that person.
2. Prepare questions for other teams.

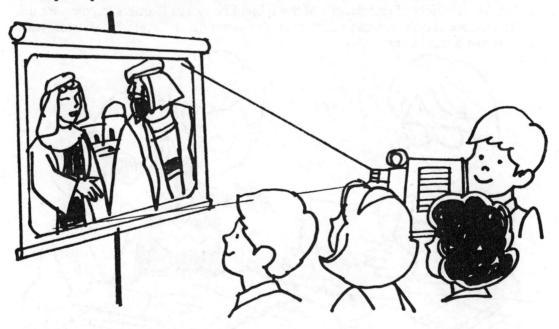

Guided Conversation Ideas
Guide learners to consider the application of Bible truth in their own lives by asking such questions as, "If you had been _____ , what would you have done? How would you feel? Do you ever feel that way now? What Bible verse(s) will help you at times like that?"

PICTURE STUDY

Purpose: That the child gain information or answer questions as he looks at pictures.

Materials
- ☐ Bibles
- ☐ Pictures (may be in books)
- ☐ Paper and pencils (optional)

Procedure
1. Picture study needs to involve looking and talking.
2. Ask the child to look at the picture(s) and (a) talk about what is happening or (b) describe the clothes Bible people are wearing or (c) name the people and tell what they are doing.
3. The content of the conversation will be determined by the picture and the specific information to be learned from it.
4. Information may be recorded on paper, or the child may immediately use the information to complete an activity.

Variations
1. Categorize and file pictures according to content or purpose. From a collection of pictures, ask the child to find all of the pictures that show a way Jesus helped someone. Place them in a designated place.
2. Look at pictures that show situations that may involve children today. Ask child to tell or show what might happen next.
3. Place pictures in sequence. For example, use several pictures that show some part of the birth of Jesus. One way to show sequence is to clip pictures to a clothesline.

Guided Conversation Ideas
"Look at these four pictures. Choose the one that shows the best thing to do when you are angry." "Look at these six pictures. Lay them on the table in a way to show what happened first and second, etc. When they are in order, clip them to the clothesline."

VIEWING/LISTENING CENTERS

Purpose: That children use a variety of materials to gain information, increase understanding and use in interacting with others.

Materials
- ☐ Listening post with headsets
- ☐ Tape recorder or record player
- ☐ Filmstrip/slide/film projector
- ☐ Books, filmstrip/slides/film
- ☐ Cassette tape or record

Procedure
1. Arrange equipment and materials before children arrive.
2. Check each piece of equipment to be certain it is working properly.
3. Sometimes the entire group will view and listen at the same time.
4. Often a small group will work at the viewing/listening center while other class members are involved in other activities. Make the center function independently by providing all directions on a sign and/or cassette tape.
5. Information, ideas and feelings gained from participating in the viewing/listening center may be used to stimulate discussion, add to information and/or assist in the completion of a Bible learning activity.

Variations
1. Teacher or children may prepare material for a viewing/listening center by recording a book on a blank cassette.
2. A response sheet can be prepared for older children to record information.

Guided Conversation Ideas
"As you view the filmstrip, list five ways to show love to others." "Listen for three things that Jesus said to His disciples."

FILMS

Purpose: That children add to ideas and information or explore feelings as they watch and listen to a film presentation.

Materials
☐ Film projector
☐ Film

Procedure
1. Preview film before class.
2. Thread projector with film. Check to see that focus and volume are set for correct viewing and listening.
3. Talk with children about what they may expect to learn. Ask questions and give specific suggestions for ideas and events to expect.
4. Follow the film with questions and discussion.
5. Information may be used to complete Bible learning activities.

Variations
1. Show a portion of the film without sound and ask the children to provide the narration or conversation.
2. Stop the film at a point of decision and ask learners what they think might happen next.
3. Show a portion of the film, then ask children to discuss what they have just seen. As they discuss, reverse projector to reshow several minutes of the film.

Guided Conversation Ideas
Conversation needs to be centered around the information, concepts and ideas presented or reinforced in the film. Question in a way that will lead children to explore their feelings about concepts.

TIME LINE

Purpose: That the learners work with time sequence in relationship to events of the Bible.

Materials
☐ Bibles
☐ Strip of newsprint or butcher paper
☐ Index cards or construction paper and felt pens
☐ Pictures (optional)

Procedure
1. List the events that are to be part of the time line.
2. Arrange them in order.
3. Divide a long strip of paper into proportional sections to represent periods of time. Write the dates in place. Write or draw the events in the correct section.

Variations
1. Prepare a time line to illustrate the seven days of creation.
2. A time line is an effective way to show the history of a mission program or of a church.
3. Children who are studying the history of the Bible will enjoy making a time line showing what they are learning.
4. Younger children can arrange pictures in sequence to tell the Bible story.
5. A time line may be used to record the progress of a current project such as the growth of a seed or bulb.
6. Collect pictures of Bible events for children to place in sequence. Christmas cards are a good source of pictures of the events surrounding the birth of Jesus.
7. Stretch a piece of yarn or clothesline across a section of the room or between two chair backs. Use spring clothespins to attach dates or pictures in the correct sequence. (See sketch for "Picture Study," page 97.)

Guided Conversation Ideas
"Who visited Jesus first, the wise men or the shepherds? What happened next? Let's talk about each picture and then put them in order to tell the story." "Write a sentence to tell about each event. Put the sentences in order to tell the story."

RESEARCH ACTIVITIES

ASSIGNMENT/PROJECT

Purpose: That the child become involved in an assignment or project that will require some research in order to complete it. For example, everyone may be asked to complete a project to tell something they think is important about Holy Week.

Materials
☐ Bibles
☐ Materials will vary according to the assignment or project. Complete the list for your project.
☐
☐
☐
☐

Procedure
1. Give clear and concise directions for completing the assignment or project.
2. Set a goal for the completion date.
3. Check at intervals to see what progress is being made.
4. Plan for a way to share the completed work with the entire group.

Variations
1. Encourage children to make some choice about the way they complete the project.
   - Some may choose to write a newspaper.
   - Some may wish to draw pictures to show Bible events.
   - Still others may decide to record imaginary interviews on a blank cassette.
2. Perhaps some children will want to complete an assignment or a project and not share it with the entire group. Allow this choice from time to time.

What will you do?	
Newspaper	Poster
1.	1.
2.	2.
3.	3.
4.	4.
Interview	Music
1.	1.
2.	2.
3.	3.
4.	4.

Guided Conversation Ideas
"How do you think _____ felt about what happened?" "What does this Bible event help us to understand about what God expects of us?"

MAP STUDY

Purpose: That learners begin to make relationships between people and events and the places where events happened.

Materials
- [ ] Bibles
- [ ] Maps
- [ ] Materials to make maps if that is an outgrowth of the study

Procedure
1. Provide maps that are related to the unit of study; for example, a map showing the missionary journeys of Paul or a map of Jerusalem showing the events of Holy Week, etc.
2. Use the maps as resource materials for Bible learning activity groups.
3. Cover maps with transparent adhesive paper; learners can then write and mark on them with washable transparency pens.

Variations
1. Learners may wish to make salt and flour maps. See "Art Activities" section, page 44 for dough recipes.
2. Maps may be traced onto acetate sheets and used on an overhead projector.
3. Use maps to increase understanding of missionary service and other places where the church is serving.
4. Simple drawings of events may be added to a map.

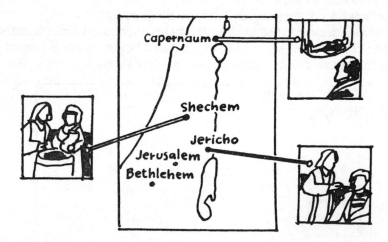

Guided Conversation Ideas
"Look at the map and scale of miles to find out how far Paul traveled. How long would that have taken?" "Let's choose some pictures to show where Jesus went during His life. Glue them to the map to show what happened where." "Where in Jerusalem were Jesus and His disciples on Thursday of Holy Week?"

MODELS, COLLECTIONS AND DISPLAYS

Purpose: That children summarize and share ideas as they use models and items of interest to create exhibits and displays.

Materials
☐ Bibles (to use as reference for labeling or checking information)
☐ Items to be displayed
☐ Display area: use boxes of different sizes to add variety to a flat table; cover area with fabric (optional)
☐ Index cards or construction paper (for signs and/or labels)
☐ Felt pens to letter signs
☐ Pictures and/or books (optional)

Procedure
1. Discuss and decide on the purpose of the display. For example, "Things God Made" or "Foods Jesus Ate." The possibilities are endless. The subject matter of the display should be related to the Scripture being studied.
2. Provide time, materials and guidance for learners to make models, collect items, letter signs and set up the display.
3. Plan a time for the display to be viewed. Other groups in the class, other classes, and parents may be involved in the learning that will occur as the display is shared.
4. An important part of preparing the display is developing a plan for sharing the information. Learners may write descriptions to place by the items. Or, they may stand near the display to answer questions and tell about the items.

Variations
1. Involve learners in field trips to collect items or gain information. For example, a simple walk around the building will yield many items from God's creation.
2. Learners may choose to make a tape recording that can be played to share information.
3. Some displays or exhibits may be attached to a bulletin board rather than being placed on a table.

Guided Conversation Ideas
Select a topic such as "Life in Bible Times." Divide it into sections and assign each section to a small group. Topics may be Food in Bible Times, Bible Times Clothes, Occupations of Bible Times, and Bible Times Buildings. Encourage groups to gather information from books, pictures, tapes, interviews, etc. Refer children to resources with comments/questions such as "What ideas does this picture give you for making a house? What materials will you need?" "This filmstrip will give you a lot of good ideas about clothing in Bible times."

FIELD TRIPS

Purpose: That children:
- gain information outside of the classroom setting;
- become involved in a service opportunity.

Materials
- ☐ Information about place to be visited
- ☐ Permission slips
- ☐ Adequate transportation
- ☐ Sufficient adult supervision

Procedure
1. Survey your community to determine the location of places that can provide meaningful information for your learners (Jewish synagogue, museum, park, police or fire station, etc.). Other places may provide opportunities for service (home for elderly or shut-in, children's home, etc.).
2. Select the place to be visited. This selection will be determined by availability and the purpose of the trip.
3. Plan and provide transportation.
4. Recruit adults to accompany the children. One adult for every four or five children is desirable.
5. Notify parents about the trip. Ask them to sign permission slips.
6. Prepare any materials needed.
7. Plan with the children so they will know what to expect.
8. Follow up the trip with discussion, evaluation and use of the information and/or experience gained.

Variations
1. Prepare a list of questions to be answered. Assign responsibility for answers to specific children.
2. Prepare a gift for persons to be visited.
3. Plan with the children for specific follow-up of the trip. For example, write letters to the shut-in visited.

Guided Conversation Ideas
"God has planned for us to show love to our neighbors. Who is our neighbor? What can we do to continue to show Mrs. Brown that we care about her?" "What did you see in the synagogue that was the same as something Jesus used in the Temple?"

BIBLE GAMES

Play and learn! Often children are not aware of the direct learning value of a game, but they participate enthusiastically because they enjoy the game. Bible games are helpful tools for involving children, in an enjoyable way, in discovering, using and remembering Bible truths and verses.

Benefits

Through Bible games the child can:
- discover new information;
- review Bible truths;
- develop skill in using the Bible and other research materials;
- reinforce skills through practice;
- build understandings;
- apply Bible truths;
- memorize Bible verses;
- increase his/her skill in interacting in a group situation (taking turns, being fair and honest).

How to Use Bible Games

Here are some beneficial ways to use Bible games:
- as a Bible readiness activity at the beginning of a Bible study unit or lesson;
- as a Bible learning activity or center;
- as a choosing activity for children who complete their work early.

Some Kinds of Games
- spinner games;
- game boards involving the movement of markers;
- game boards based on a known game such as football, hopscotch, etc.;
- pocket games;
- team games;
- individual games;
- known games with Bible information (tic-tac-toe);
- game with little or no competition;
- table games;
- choice games;
- review games.

Selecting, Constructing and Storing Games
1. Decide what your purpose is in using a Bible game. For example, do you want children to *discover* information, *review* information, or *apply* information?
2. Select a game that will help you accomplish your purpose. (Note that each of the games on the following pages has a stated purpose.)
3. Adapt the game according to the Bible content you are studying and the abilities and needs of your students.
4. Keep the game procedures and rules simple. Type or letter them on a card and tape them in an appropriate place on the game board, or put them on the game envelope.
5. See supply list on page 6 for basic supplies for making games.
6. Protect game parts with clear plastic.
7. Store games in shallow, flat drawers or boxes.

Tips
1. Construct some basic game boards that can be used with a number of teaching units by changing the content you put on the game cards.
2. Involve parents and other interested adults in collecting material for making games. Invite them to a game-making work session.
3. Encourage children to make games for other groups to use. They also enjoy making games and game cards to use themselves.
4. Use Bible games from your curriculum materials. Some additional games are suggested on the following pages.

CONCENTRATION

Purpose: That children:
- discover or review Bible facts;
- match Bible verses with references;
- match two parts of a Bible verse;
- match Bible verses with life application.

Materials
☐ Pairs of index cards with information related to unit of study; mark each matching pair of cards with the same symbol as a self-check feature. Examples of kinds of information that can be matched:
- Questions/answers
- Bible verses/references
- First part of verse/last part of verse
- Bible words/pictures
- Bible words/brief definitions
- Bible people/events
- Bible places/events
- Book of Bible/writer or event in book
- Daily problem/Bible verse related to the problem

Use 5 or 6 pairs of cards for first and second graders. Use 10 to 12 pairs for older children.

Players
Two to six. A larger group requires too much time waiting for turns.

Procedure
1. Mix up index cards and place them face down on table or floor.
2. The first player turns two cards face up so everyone can see them. If they match, he/she keeps them and takes another turn. If not he/she turns them over again, and the next player takes a turn.
3. The child with the most cards at the end of the game is the winner.

Variation
For younger children, make duplicate word, verse or picture cards. Children look for cards that are the same.

TIC-TAC-TOE

Purpose: To discover and/or review Bible information.

Materials
☐ Bibles
☐ Tic-tac-toe framework
Draw framework on paper or poster board. Or use any of these variations:
- masking tape on floor or table
- yarn on flannelboard

(continued on next page)

☐ Five X markers; five 0 markers

Use a felt pen to mark X or O on squares of cardboard or felt.

☐ Game cards

Write on small index cards questions related to unit of study (one question per card). Give Bible reference where answer can be found.

Players

Two to 10. If more than two children play, divide the group into two teams. Players on teams take turns answering questions.

Procedure

1. First player chooses a question card, reads it aloud and gives the answer.
   - If answer is correct, player places an X or O marker on any square.
   - If answer is incorrect, player forfeits chance to put a marker on game board. Opponent may answer same question or take a new question card.
2. Players continue to take turns until one player has three markers in a row (in any direction), thus becoming the winner.

BIBLE FOOTBALL

Purpose: To discover and/or review Bible information.

Materials

☐ Bible
☐ Football field game board drawn on poster board (see sketch)

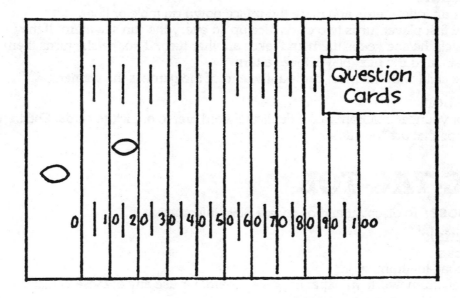

(continued on next page)

☐ Game cards

Write on small index cards questions related to unit of study (one question per card). Use different colors for 5-, 10-, 15- and 20-yard questions (5-yard questions are the easiest, 20-yard questions are the hardest). Give Bible reference where answer can be found.

☐ Two "football" markers (one per team)

Use buttons or other small objects.

Players

Eight to 10. Play in teams of four or five.

Procedure

1. Teams take turns drawing game cards. (Decide ahead of time whether cards are to be drawn at random or according to each player's choice as to difficulty.)
2. Player answers question and checks answer in the Bible.
3. If answer is correct, player moves his/her team's marker the appropriate number of yards.
4. The team reaching the goal line first wins.

BIBLE BASEBALL

Purpose, materials and number of players is the same as for Bible Football, with these exceptions:

● Use a baseball game board.
● Prepare one-base, two-base, three-base and home-run questions.

Play and score (runs and outs) as in baseball.

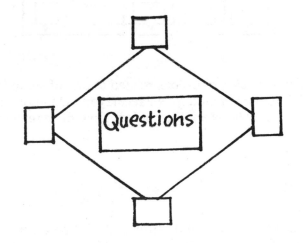

BIBLE JEOPARDY

Purpose: That children review or discover Bible facts.

Materials
☐ Bibles
☐ Jeopardy game board (see sketch)
- Mark five columns on poster board (one for each category).
- Use paper clips or a reusable adhesive material to fasten category topics as in sketch.
- Tape five strips of cardboard as in sketch to make pockets for holding game cards. Number strips as in sketch to show number of points that can be earned by answering the question.

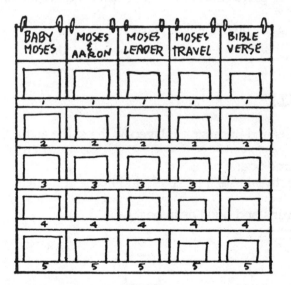

☐ Game cards

Write on small index cards questions related to unit of study (one question per card). Use a different color card for each category. One-point questions are the easiest; five-point questions are the hardest. Give Bible reference where answer can be found.

Players
Four to six.

Procedure
1. First player selects a category and game card. He/she answers question and checks answer in Bible.
2. If answer is correct, player scores the number of points assigned to that question.
3. Each player keeps his/her own score.

BIBLE GAMES

STRING-A-MATCH

Purpose: That children match Bible people with:
- events in their lives
- their occupations
- a related Bible verse.

Materials
- ☐ Bible
- ☐ Game board (see sketch)
  Use information related to your unit of study. Connect correct answers with yarn or shoelaces.

Born Again ● (John 3:3)	● To die or to be lost from God and His love.
	● Living forever in God's presence.
Eternal Life ● (John 3:16)	● To be so convinced that Jesus is God that we follow His commands; to completely trust Jesus to forgive our sins.
Pharisee ● (John 3:1)	
Believe in Him ● (John 3:16)	● Begin a new life spiritually; become members of God's family.
Perish ● (John 3:16)	● Important religious leaders who emphasized obeying all details of Jewish law.
Condemn ● (John 3:17)	● To declare someone is wrong or guilty and deserving of punishment.

Players
One or two.

Procedure
1. Players take turns matching questions and names.
2. They check their answers in the Bible.

MATCH STICKS

Purpose: That children match:
- questions and answers;
- Bible verses and references;
- Bible people and events.

Materials:
☐ Bible
☐ Tongue depressors or Popsicle or craft sticks
Prepare pairs of matching sticks by writing on them:
- a question / the answer
- a Bible verse / the reference
- a Bible person / a related event.

Players
One to four.

Procedure
1. Players take turns finding two sticks that match.
2. They check their answers in the Bible.

THROW-CATCH-ANSWER

Purpose: That children respond verbally to review questions about their Bible lessons.

Materials
☐ Bibles
☐ Prepared list of unit-related questions
☐ Nerf ball

Players
Eight to 10.

Procedure
1. Children sit in a circle.
2. Start the game by tossing the Nerf ball to a player. If the player catches the ball, he/she tries to answer the question you ask. If player is correct, he/she throws the Nerf ball to another player who tries to answer the next question. Encourage players to involve everyone in the circle.

Variation
Have children list ahead of time several questions they want to ask. They ask their own questions when it's their turn to throw the Nerf ball.

SPIN AND GO

Purpose: That children discover/review Bible information.

Materials
☐ Bibles
☐ Path game board (as illustrated or as you design)
☐ Markers (for example, buttons) to move around board—one per player
☐ Unit-related questions on small index cards
    Include reference of verse where answer can be found.
☐ Spinner
    Use a spinner from a commercial game or make one as illustrated, using
    lightweight cardboard and a paper fastener.

Note: School supply stores usually carry packaged game parts such as spinners,
markers and blank re-usable game cards.

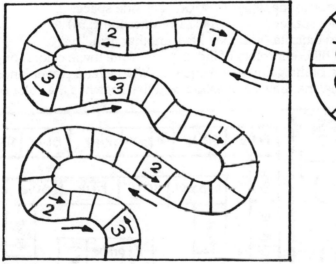 

Variation
Add variety by placing a small dot (use different colors) on some of the spaces.
When a player stops on that spot, he/she does what the color indicates. For
example:
- blue = go back to the beginning
- yellow = take another turn
- red = go back two spaces
- green = move ahead two spaces

Players
Four to six.

Procedure
1. Each player, in turn, takes a question, answers it and checks answer in Bible.
2. If answer is correct, player spins the spinner and moves the number of spaces
   indicated by the spinner.

SPIN A BIBLE FACT

Purpose: That children discover/review Bible facts.

Materials
- ☐ Bibles
- ☐ Game board (see illustration)
- ☐ Markers (for example, buttons) to move around board—one per player
- ☐ Unit-related questions on small index cards (plus Bible reference for checking answer)
- ☐ Spinner (from a commercial game or made as illustrated, using lightweight cardboard and a paper fastener)

Variations
1. Written directions that can be used in game board squares:
   - Skip your turn.
   - Stop! Name a book in the Bible.
   - Move ahead three spaces.
   - Spin again.
   - Go back one space.
   - ? (for question card)
2. Use gummed stickers to indicate "you may have another turn."
3. Write questions on two different colors of index cards. Write these colors (or glue colored cards) on some of the game board squares. Whenever a player lands on one of these squares, he/she draws a question card that matches the color on that square.

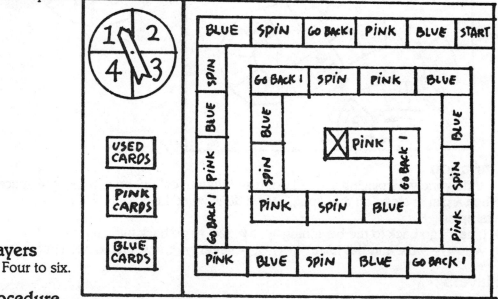

Players
Four to six.

Procedure
1. Each player, in turn, spins the spinner and moves to the appropriate square. He/she follows the directions in that square.
2. If a player draws a question card and gives correct answer, he/she stays on that square. If the correct answer is not given, player must return marker to square it was on at the beginning of that turn.

SURPRISE PICTURE

Purpose: That children:
- identify a Bible event/lesson as a small strip of the lesson picture is revealed;
- locate and read the related portion of Scripture.

Materials
- ☐ Bibles
- ☐ Large envelope with strips cut as in illustration
- ☐ Unit-related Bible story pictures to insert in envelope
  Add to each picture the Bible reference (no more than one or two verses) for checking answer.

Can you name the picture?
Find it in your Bible. Read about it.

Players
Four to six.

Procedure
1. Players, in turn, choose a strip to be opened and try to identify the Bible event from as much of the picture as can be seen at that time.
2. The player who makes an identification is further challenged to locate and read the Bible verses that tell about the event.

Variation
Put a picture in large envelope and pull it out an inch at a time.

ADD-A-NUMBER

Purpose: That children:
- discover/review Bible information;
- estimate skill by selecting difficulty of question.

Materials
☐ Bibles
☐ Game board (see illustration)
☐ Question cards

   Write one unit-related question on each index card (use different colors to indicate each level of difficulty: five-point questions are hardest; two-point questions are easiest). Include Bible reference for checking answer.

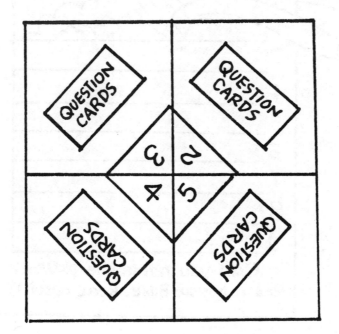

Players
   Four to six.

Procedure
1. Each player, in turn, draws a card from the question stack in one section of the game board and answers it.
2. If answer is correct, player adds to his/her score the number of points indicated.

SORTING GAME

Purpose: That children sort given information into categories.

Materials
☐ Bibles
☐ Resource books
☐ Game board with pockets (see illustration)
   Use library pockets or envelopes. Fasten category names to pockets with a re-usable adhesive. Use as many pockets as needed.
☐ Game cards (small index cards) with information to be sorted. Include Bible reference (or page of another resource) to use in checking answers. Some ideas for categories and cards:

Categories	Game Cards
Bible places	Bible events
Bible people	Facts about people
Days of Creation	What God created
Old Testament/New Testament	OT/NT events
Divisions of the Bible	Bible books

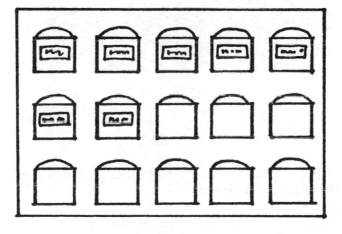

Variation
Use small boxes on a table (or the floor) instead of a pocket-type game board.

Players
Four to six.

Procedure
1. Distribute game cards to players.
2. Each player, in turn, places his/her card in the correct pocket and then checks Bible or other resource for accuracy of answer.

BIBLE WORD GAME

Purpose: That children identify key Bible words in a lesson or unit.

Materials
☐ Bible
☐ Game board similar to Scrabble (see illustration)
☐ Paper
☐ Pencils

Players
Two to four.

Procedure
1. Each player, working independently, makes a list of 15 unit-related Bible words (names of people, places and objects).
2. Choose a scorekeeper.
3. The first player chooses a word from his/her list and letters it on game board, one letter to a square. Player scores one point for each letter in the word.
4. Next player letters a word which contains one of the letters in the first word.
5. Players continue to add words similarly. A word may be used only once. Words may be placed horizontally or vertically. Letters do not have to spell a word in all directions.
6. Game continues in this manner until board is filled or time is expired. Player with the most points wins.

Variations
1. Cover game board with clear plastic. Players use washable transparency pens to letter words. Board can be wiped off and re-used again.
2. Use Anagram letters to spell words.

STRING-A-VERSE

Purpose: That children:
- connect the words of a Bible verse in the correct sequence;
- use the Bible to check their sequence of words;
- increase their understanding of the verse through discussion while working with the game.

Materials
☐ Bible
☐ Cards with scrambled Bible verses. Put a paper fastener at the beginning of each word on the card. Tie one end of a piece of yarn to the first paper fastener.

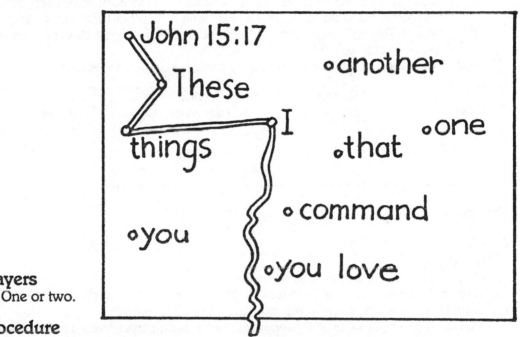

Players
One or two.

Procedure
1. Player strings yarn around heads of paper fasteners to show correct sequence of words.
2. Player checks Bible to determine accuracy of his/her work.
3. Encourage child to tell the meaning of the verse in his/her own words and to memorize the verse.

Variations
1. Children in grades 4-6 enjoy preparing cards for one another.
2. To add interest for older children, use a stop watch to time the completion of the verse.
3. Instead of using yarn and paper fasteners, you can put a dot in front of each word and then cover the card with clear plastic. Let children use washable transparency pens to connect words. Their lines can be wiped off, making the card re-usable.

PASS IT ON

Purpose: That children:
- become familiar with Bible verses they will be studying during the unit;
- show their knowledge of a unit-related Bible verse by arranging phrases in the correct sequence.

Materials
☐ Bible
☐ Game cards (four small index cards per Bible verse)
   Divide Bible verse (including reference) into four parts; letter or type one part of verse on each card. Put the same symbol or letter at the bottom of each card to show that these cards go together. Do the same with other Bible verses in your unit of study. You will need as many Bible verses as you have players playing the game at one time.
☐ Box or envelope in which to store game cards. Label it "Pass It On."

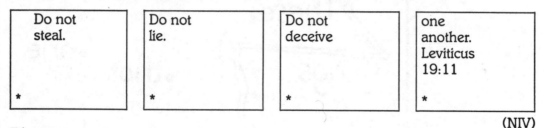

(NIV)

Players
Three to six.

Procedure
1. Players sit in a circle at a table or on the floor.
2. Use cards for as many Bible verses as there are players. One player (called the leader) shuffles cards and gives four cards to each player.
3. Players hold cards so others cannot see them. Each player checks to see if his/her cards make a verse. The object of the game is to be the first person to put a verse together correctly and say, "I made a verse."
4. Leader says, "Ready, set, pass it on." Each player passes one card he/she does not wish to keep, face down, to the player on the right.
5. When a player's cards make a complete verse, he/she places cards face up on table or rug, in the correct order.
6. Players check verse in Bible to see if the order is correct.
7. The game continues until all verses are assembled or as time allows.

BIBLE LINKO

Purpose: That child:
● become familiar with Bible verses;
● show his/her knowledge of the verse by helping put it together in the correct order.

Materials
☐ Bible
☐ Game cards
  Cut about 50 tagboard cards 2x2-inches (5x5 cm). Use these cards to make several copies of a Bible verse and reference. Letter one word per card, including punctuation with closest word.
☐ Box or envelope in which to store game cards. Label it "Bible Linko—(reference of verse)."

For	the	Son	of	man	has	come

to	save	that	which	was	lost.

Matthew	18:11	For	the	Son	of	man

Players
Three to six.

Procedure
1. Player 1 reads the Bible verse and chooses someone to tell what it means.
2. Player 1 mixes up the cards and then gives each player an equal number, putting some extras face down on the table.
3. Each player looks at his/her cards but doesn't show them to anyone else.
4. Player 1 places one card face up. The player to his/her right tries to put a word card from his/her pile before or after this word. For example in the verse "For the son of man is. . .," the card "man" might be played first. The next player needs to place "of" before or "is" after "man." Children can check verse in the Bible as often as needed.
5. If this player cannot play a word, he/she may exchange one card with the "extras" pile. If this player is still not able to play, he/she "passes."
6. The game continues with the next player. The winner is the person who plays all (or most) of his/her cards.

BIBLE VERSE INLAY

Purpose: That children manipulate words in a Bible verse while its meaning and application are being discussed.

Materials
☐ Bible
☐ Bible verse inlay boards (see illustration)
Letter the Bible verse on poster board. Cut out a variety of shapes—one around each word. Glue this cutout board to a solid piece of poster board of the same size.

Players
One student for each verse. A small group of four to six may play at the same time, using related Bible verses from their unit of study.

Procedure
1. Children complete the Bible verse by putting the words in the correct places on the board. (The shapes of the word cards are clues for children who have difficulty in reading and sequence.) As the children work, talk about the meaning and application of the verse.
2. Children take the word cards out of the inlay board and try to arrange them in the correct order without using the board. They use their Bibles to check the accuracy of their work.
3. Encourage children to try to say the verse without looking at the words.

SCRAMBLED VERSE

Purpose: That child:
- become familiar with unit Bible verses;
- show his/her knowledge of Bible verses by putting the words in the correct order.

Materials
☐ Bible
☐ Scrambled Bible verses
- Letter each Bible verse and reference on a small envelope. (Lettering each phrase on a new line aids meaning and memorization.)
- Letter each Bible verse on an index card or tagboard. Cut words apart; put them in the appropriate envelope.

Note: Using a different color card and/or ink for each verse helps children keep the right words with the right verse when several verses are being used.

Players
One student for each verse. A small group of four to six may play at the same time, using related Bible verses from their unit of study.

Procedure
1. Children choose an envelope and take the cards out.
2. If the verse is unfamiliar to them, they put the cards in the correct order while looking at the verse in their Bible or on the envelope.
3. When children are familiar with the verse, they mix the cards up and see if they can put the words in the correct order without looking at the verse in their Bible or on the envelope. They may check the verse as often as they need help.
4. Encourage children to continue working on the verse until they can put the entire verse together correctly without help.

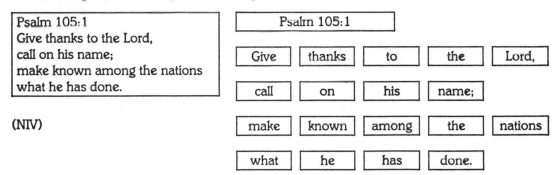

Psalm 105:1
Give thanks to the Lord,
call on his name;
make known among the nations
what he has done.

(NIV)

Psalm 105:1

Give	thanks	to	the	Lord,
call	on	his	name;
make	known	among	the	nations
what	he	has	done.

Variations
1. For beginning readers, record the verse on tape so children can listen to the verse as they read it on the envelope—thus becoming familiar with any new words.
2. For younger children—or with long verses—cut some parts of the verse into

(continued on next page)

groups of words (e.g., phrases) instead of single words.

3. To encourage children to work on more than one verse, make "how many can you do" cards (see illustration). Put a number on each Bible verse envelope. Children check that number on their cards when they can complete the verse without help.

4. Letter the verse and reference on larger cardboard and cut the words apart to make cards for playing "Treasure Hunt." Before class, you or a student hide the word cards (in fairly obvious places) in one section of the room. Children see if they can find all the words and put them in the correct order. They can use their Bibles as they work. When verse is completed they use the Bible to check the accuracy of their work.

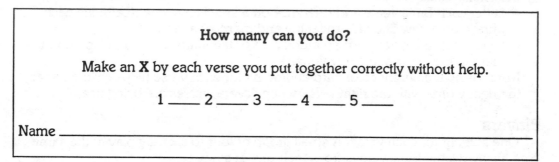

BIBLE VERSE SHAPE PUZZLES

Purpose: That children:
- place words of a Bible verse in the correct order while talking about its meaning and applications;
- tell how the shape of the completed puzzle helps them understand or remember the verse.

Materials
☐ Bible
☐ Bible verse puzzles (see illustration)
  Design puzzle pieces to make a shape that relates to the meaning of the verse.

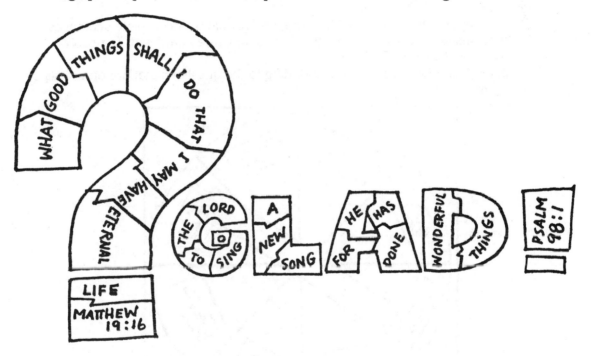

Players
One player for each verse. A small group of four to six may play at the same time, using related Bible verses from their unit of study. Occasionally, children will enjoy working together in pairs.

Procedure
1. Child puts Bible verse puzzle together and checks in the Bible.
2. Talk about the meaning and application of the verse. Discuss significance of shape.
3. Encourage memorization by having child remove a few words at a time and say verse without the help of those words.

SPINNER GAME

Purpose: That children:
- discover and/or review Bible information;
- work with Bible verses;
- discuss present-day situations and the application of Bible truth to those situations.

Materials
- ☐ Bible
- ☐ Spinner game board (see illustration)
  Make board and spinner arrow out of sturdy poster board. Fasten with paper fastener.
- ☐ Slips of paper with unit-related information (questions, incomplete sentences, Bible verses with words left out, etc.) Fasten to game board with re-usable adhesive or paper clips.
- ☐ Resource materials needed for responding to the questions that are on the slips of paper.

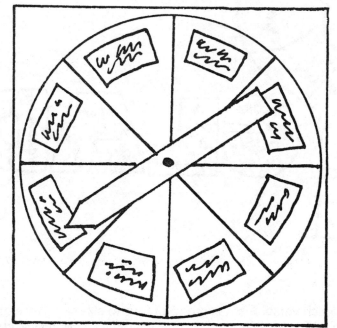

Players
Four to six.

Procedure
1. Each player, in turn, spins the spinner and responds to the item that is in the section where the spinner stops.
2. Player uses Bible and resource materials needed for information and/or checking answers.

SECRET CODE

Purpose: That children:
- discover new information in an interesting way (decoding it);
- discuss the meaning and application of Bible verses.

Materials
- [ ] Bible
- [ ] Several secret code cards (see illustration)
- [ ] Large index cards on which you have written in code a message to be decoded.
  - Bible verse (include uncoded reference so child can check his/her answer)
  - Definition of a new Bible word or phrase
  - Information about a Bible times custom.

  Be sure to space out symbols so there is plenty of room to write letters under them. Leave extra space between words. (See illustration.)
- [ ] Paper
- [ ] Pencils
- [ ] Paper clips (optional)

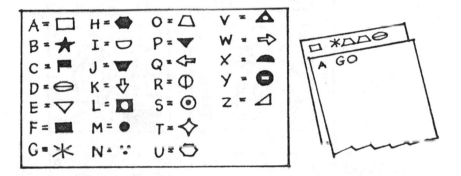

Players
One per coded message (or children can work in pairs—one finding the correct letter, the other writing it down).

Procedure
1. Child places paper below row of symbols and writes the correct letters after checking the code card. (See illustration.) Clip paper to card for use by younger children.
2. Child checks answer in the Bible (or on the back of the card).

Variations
1. Use numerals rather than symbols.
2. Vary the symbols used; number the codes: Code 1, Code 2, etc. On the coded message card, identify which code to use.

70302

CLOTHESPIN BIBLE VERSES

Purpose: That children match Bible verses with Bible lesson pictures and present-day pictures.

Materials
☐ Bible
☐ Collection of pictures attached to poster board (see illustration)
☐ Clothespins with Bible verses and/or Bible references glued to them or written on them.

Players
Four to six.

Procedure
1. Children use Bibles to read and talk about the Bible verses that are on the clothespins.
2. They match each Bible verse to the appropriate picture by clipping it to the edge of the poster board.
3. They tell why they chose that verse for that picture.